A Biblical Pattern of Prayer: Exploring Prayer in the Old Testament

Jennifer Anne Cox

Published by Jennifer Anne Cox, 2023.

While every precaution has been taken in the preparation of this book, the publisher assumes no responsibility for errors or omissions, or for damages resulting from the use of the information contained herein.

A BIBLICAL PATTERN OF PRAYER: EXPLORING PRAYER IN THE OLD TESTAMENT

First edition. September 29, 2023.

ISBN: 979-8223324454

Written by Jennifer Anne Cox.

Contents

Introduction

<hr>

In mid-2022 I visited a friend for a catch-up. On the way there I decided to occupy myself by thinking about something. That something was prayer. As I drove, I thought and prayed at the same time about prayer. I asked many questions about prayer. Why does God ask us to pray? Why does he sometimes answer prayer quickly, sometimes takes a long time, and sometimes seemingly not at all? How should we pray? I can point to some amazing answers to prayer in my own life and some prayers that have not yet been answered after months or years. Perhaps you also have questions. I wish that I could answer all the questions about prayer. I would be lying if I said that I had figured this all out.

This is not the first book I have written about prayer. The first book—*Prayer: Not the Right Words but the Right God[1]*—is based on the idea that there is no magic formula to get God to listen to us. Jesus Christ alone is the secret to prayer. We must come to God through him and him alone. I decided to write a second book on prayer, not because I understand prayer, but because I do not understand prayer. I want to grasp how to pray in a biblical way. I hope this book will move that goal forward. Even so, I am sure that there is much more to be understood.

In this book, I consider what the Old Testament has to tell us about prayer, both through prayers people prayed in its pages and through what the authors teach directly about prayer. Although it might be possible to include every prayer in the Old Testament, this comprehensiveness might prove tedious. Consequently, particular incidents and particular people and their prayers have been included while others have been left out. The goal is to learn the lessons we

<hr>

1. *https://www.smashwords.com/books/view/1115958*

are taught in these narratives, in the law and the prophets. It is not necessary to include every single detail in order to do this.

Not every book of the Bible contains prayers or a theology of prayer. On the other hand, one book in the Old Testament is full of prayers—prayers of individuals and prayers written for the congregation to pray together. That is the book of Psalms. Because this is a treasure-trove of prayer in itself, it deserves a book or more of its own. For this reason, I have not included Psalms in my exploration of prayer in the Old Testament. This may be a project in the future, along with considering prayer in the New Testament.

To help you understand where this book is heading, the simplest statement about what the Old Testament says about prayer is this. God speaks to human beings (in person or in his written word) and humans respond in prayer. Prayer to the living God is a response to God's words, covenant, redemptive actions and promises. This is true whether the prayer is one of praise, repentance, petition, intercession or a cry for mercy.

Although I will no doubt repeat this point within the chapters, it is important to clarify what I mean by God's word to us. God's word to us is a misunderstood concept in the church today. There are examples of God speaking directly to people in the Bible. This was particularly true in the early books of the Bible. At that point, if God were to reveal himself to humans, he had to do this directly since no Bible existed. As the Bible progresses, the people in the Bible are able to rely more on God's written word. After Moses, the first five books of the Bible existed, and the people of Israel could know God's character through this record. If they wanted to know God's promises or what is right or wrong, they could refer to what God had already said. As for Christians, we have the complete Bible to give us understanding of God, his redemptive actions, his character, his promises and his commands. This does not, I believe, exclude the possibility of God speaking directly in prophecy (for example). However, when I say that prayer is a response to God's word to us, I refer to his written word in the Bible rather than any subjective experience that seems like God speaking.

The whole Bible is about Jesus Christ and points us towards him and our need for him (John 5:39). This book focuses on the prayers of the Old Testament, but my intention is to still keep Jesus at the centre of the discussion. The coming of Christ brought about a radical change for God's people. The way in which Christians relate to God is not the same as the way in which the Old Testament saints did so. Prayer is still prayer, but Christians do not need to offer blood sacrifices or approach God in the physical temple building. Neither are their mediatorial offices (kings, prophets and priests) in the church in the same way there were in ancient Israel. Christ alone is our mediator (see *Jesus Christ, the One Mediator between God and Humanity*[2] for more details) and this impacts the way we pray. For this reason, I have sought to point out both the similarities and differences between prayer under the old covenant and prayer under the new covenant.

Generally speaking, this book moves through the Bible in the order of the biblical canon, that is, in the order that the books of the Bible usually appear. On occasion I deviate from this rule, such as when I refer to the prayers of women, occasions where there are parallel passages, or in regard to the minor prophets. As always, I encourage you to read passages for yourself and to check their context, to be sure that what I have said is correct.

In order to help the reader to apply a biblical pattern of prayer to her or his life, each chapter contains some reflection questions at the end of the chapter. These could be used as journal prompts, for personal

---

2. *https://www.smashwords.com/books/view/1057125*

consideration or for group discussion. The reader may want to go slowly through the book, reading only a chapter at a time and pondering the implications for a personal prayer life.

Foundations: Genesis 1–3

Genesis, particularly the first few chapters, is foundational to Old Testament theology and therefore the theology of the New Testament. God's creation of humanity in his image and likeness provides a basis for prayer. Genesis 1 and 2 offer us two complementary accounts of the creation of humanity. Genesis 1 contains the big picture of God as Creator and his relationship to human beings. Genesis 2 focuses on Adam (and later Eve) in the garden with God. Genesis 3 provides an explanation of how humanity's relationship with God became broken. Humans were made to pray to their Creator, but sin changed prayer and distorted it into something it should not be.

Humans Were Made for Relationship with God

After the initial creation of the heavens and the earth by God, God shaped the world: light, sky, sea, vegetation, sun and moon (Gen 1:1–19). Then God populated the world with living creatures: water creatures, winged creatures and land animals (Gen 1:20–25). Each of these creatures have their place in the world and are called "good" by God. However, the creation of human beings made it clear that humans are distinct and different to the other living creatures in the world.

> Then God said, "Let us make man in our image, after our likeness. And let them have dominion over the fish of the sea and over the birds of the heavens and over the livestock and over all the earth and over every creeping thing that creeps on the earth." So God created man in his own image, in the image of God he created him; male and female he created them. (Gen 1:26–27)

Although humans share with other living creatures the fact that they are created, they are special in terms of their relationship with the Creator. Only humans are called the image of God (not even angels are called this). Is not necessary in this context to get into the details of what this image entails, but only to say that being in the image of God sets human beings apart as creatures who have been given a purposeful and unique relationship with God. This truth applies equally to both male and female humans (Gen 1:27).

In the act of creation, it is obvious that the initiative lay with God and with no one else. There was nothing and then God made something. No person existed outside of the Trinity to suggest to God that he create the universe. Thus, the existence of human beings is exclusively the result of God's decision. Therefore, the relationship between God and human beings has God's initiative as its basis. It was not a human decision to have relationship with God. God determined that he would make humans in his image and that is what he did. Prayer is part of human relationship with God. But prayer does not begin with us. God takes the initiative in relationship to humans and therefore he is the initiator of prayer as well.

Genesis 2 gives us a more detailed picture of God and humanity in the Garden of Eden. After the world was prepared, "then the LORD God formed the man of dust from the ground and breathed into his nostrils the breath of life, and the man became a living creature" (Gen 2:7). The creation of the first human was not done at a distance. God himself breathed into the creature of dust and gave him life. This is a picture of the deep and intimate communion with God that humans were made for. Given such a beginning, how could Adam not desire conversation with his Creator? Prayer was possible because of God's closeness to his human creatures. Prayer would have been sweet in the Garden of Eden, without restriction or distortion.

The whole earth and all the heavens were created by God, but God made a place where Adam (and later Eve) would live, a garden. Adam (with Eve) was given charge of the garden, to work it and keep it (Gen 2:15). Many theologians believe that the Garden of Eden was the first temple on earth. A temple is a place where God is present, and there people can meet with God and worship him. In the Garden of Eden, Adam and Eve were created to dwell with God, to know him and to worship him. Although no words of humans to God are recorded in chapters 1 and 2, we can assume that in the garden temple, God intended that humans call upon their Creator.

The worship in the Garden involved deliberate obedience to God's commands. In both versions of the creation narrative, God spoke and gave the humans commands to keep. Specifically, in Gen 2 the command is as follows. "And the LORD God commanded the man, saying, 'You may surely eat of every tree of the garden, but of the tree of the knowledge of good and evil you shall not eat, for in the day that you eat of it you shall surely die'" (Gen 2:16–17). Adam and Eve were to enjoy the garden and the provision within it, because God wanted them to be cared for even before they cared for the garden. But there was one tree that was forbidden. As God's creatures, what Adam and Eve did should have been based upon the word of God. If they had done so, this would have been acceptable worship (compare Rom 12:1–2). Sadly, this is not what happened.

Sin Ruined Everything

We don't know how long Adam and Eve were in the state of paradise in the Garden. But at some point, possibly very soon after they were created, the serpent came into the garden and spoke with Eve. "Now the serpent was more crafty than any other beast of the field that the LORD God had made. He said to the woman, 'Did God actually say, "You shall not eat of any tree in the garden"?'" (Gen 3:1). The serpent represents an embodied devil (Rev 12:9). Eve would not have known that, but we can reasonably assume that a serpent talking about what God had said should have thrown up a red flag for Eve.

The sad fact is that Eve engaged in a back-and-forth conversation with this serpent, and this resulted in her fall into sin (Gen 3:1–6). This story provides us with a concrete example of a failure to pray. God was available to the first humans. He could have explained to Eve this commandment if she had asked him. If she felt unsure of what to do with a talking serpent, Eve could have easily prayed for God's help and God would have immediately helped her. Yet, instead of trusting the word of God given to Adam and passed on to her, she thought it would not hurt to disobey it. Eve might have been the first person to eat of the forbidden tree, but Adam did the same immediately after her (Gen 3:6). Neither of them prayed about this temptation. Neither of them turned to God for aid or wisdom.

The situation then changed for the worse. After they had succumbed to temptation and eaten the forbidden fruit, they first tried to hide their nakedness and then they tried to hide from their Creator, as he walked in the garden with them (Gen 3:7–8). The LORD God was present with his people, but sin had made that presence terrifying. Even so, at that point it would have been possible to own up to what they had done and to repent of their sin. God was not far from them. He had not yet banished the humans from his garden temple. But the first people did not repent. Prayer was not their go-to.

Instead, it was God who spoke to the humans.

> But the LORD God called to the man and said to him, "Where are you?" And he said, "I heard the sound of you in the garden, and I was afraid, because I was naked, and I hid myself." He said, "Who told you that you were naked? Have you eaten of the tree of which I commanded you not to eat?"

The man said, "The woman whom you gave to be with me, she gave me fruit of the tree, and I ate." Then the LORD God said to the woman, "What is this that you have done?" The woman said, "The serpent deceived me, and I ate." (Gen 3:9–13)

The initiative was again with God and the humans responded. If we define prayer as speaking to God, then prayer actually took place here in response to God's questions. It was not a positive experience for these now-sinful humans. Neither asked God for forgiveness. Adam blamed the woman for his sin, and indeed mentioning "the woman you gave to be with me" was an indirect way of blaming God for his sin. The woman blamed the serpent for her sin. Neither of them accepted the blame for failing to believe God's word to them. But this story shows us a pattern that will appear many times in the Old Testament. God took the initiative and spoke to the people. He sought relationship with the two sinners.

Sin changed prayer. The man and the woman were barred from the Garden of Eden (Gen 3:22–24), or to put that another way, they were barred from the temple in which God's presence dwells. This did not mean that prayer ceased to exist in the world. However, now a distance between people and God exists were none existed before. After the fall and expulsion from Eden this distance grew greater as sin increased.

Conclusion

God created human beings to be in relationship with him. We were always intended to pray to our Creator. We have no positive examples of prayer in Gen 1–3, only an absence of prayer when prayer was desperately needed, and prayer that lacked repentance after the fall. However, because God made humans to be special creatures, greater than the rest of creation, we can be sure that prayer and worship of God would have been a normal part of human life if sin had not changed humanity for the worst. In the absence of sin, humans would have prayed to God regularly and often, thanking him for his goodness, praising his glory, and asking him for wisdom. But sin's effects included the disruption of these functions of prayer (see Rom 1:18–23).

Reflection Questions / Journal Prompts

1. Meditate on the wonder of being made for relationship with God.
2. What difference does it make to your understanding of prayer that God takes the initiative in prayer?
3. Consider the different ways in which sin in your life affects how you pray or don't pray.

Genesis 4–50: God's Redemptive Activity Begins

S in is a huge problem for prayer, but God is neither passive nor helpless. He promised a redeemer even in the midst of pronouncing judgement on the serpent in the Garden. "I will put enmity between you and the woman, and between your offspring and her offspring; he shall bruise your head, and you shall bruise his heel" (Gen 3:15). We know that the fulfilment of this promise awaited the coming of Christ to defeat the devil through his own death on the cross. That occurred thousands of years after the fall. Nonetheless, God's redemptive plan began in Genesis. Even as sin grew worse, he worked to make a people for himself.

Cain, Abel and Seth: Righteousness Continued

The contrast between those who know God and those who prefer sin was first evidenced in the lives of Adam and Eve's sons Cain and Abel. Both Cain and Abel brought offerings to God, but the LORD accepted Abel's offering and not Cain's. Cain was angry and murdered his brother (Gen 4:1–8). Yet God offered Cain an opportunity for repentance. "Then the LORD said to Cain, 'Where is Abel your brother?' He said, 'I do not know; am I my brother's keeper?'" (Gen 4:9). Cain failed to ask God for mercy or forgiveness and only spoke to God to complain about his punishment. Even so, the LORD mitigated his punishment by marking Cain to prevent him being killed (Gen 4:10–15). But the end result was that "Cain went away from the presence of the LORD and settled in the land of Nod, east of Eden" (Gen 4:16). Adam and Eve had been expelled from the Garden of

Eden, the place of intimacy with God. But Cain's sin cast him even further from the Garden temple and away from God's presence.

The story leaves us wondering about the depths to which humanity had fallen in such a short time. Would prayer ever be offered to God when humans were in this dreadful state of sin? Prayer seems an unlikely outcome of these events. However, God gave Eve another son, who was called Seth. Seth grew and had a son of his own (Gen 4:25–26a). "At that time people began to call upon the name of the LORD" (Gen 4:26b). The unrighteous line extended through Cain (Gen 4:17–24), but a righteous line was given by God through Seth, one that would eventually lead to the Messiah. It was this righteous line who called upon the LORD, no doubt with prayer and praise. Despite the poor start in Gen 1–4 in regard to prayer, all was not lost. In this instance the catalyst for prayer was not a word from God but the action of replacing righteous Abel (the first martyr—see Matt 23:35; Luke 11:51; Heb 11:4) with another righteous man, Seth.

Noah: Inadvertent Intercessor

Following the story of Cain and Abel is the genealogy of Adam, which ends with Noah and his sons. It is not surprising, then, that the story of Noah is very significant. God was grieved by the fact that his world was filled with wicked human beings, and he decided to wipe them off the face of the earth and begin again (Gen 6:1–7). One man was different. "But Noah found favour in the eyes of the LORD. ... Noah was a righteous man, blameless in his generation. Noah walked with God" (Gen 6:8–9, abridged). Noah was a man obedient to God, according to God's word as it had been revealed by that point in history. When God commanded Noah to build an ark to preserve pairs of animals and his own family (eight in all) Noah's response was obedience (Gen 6: 9–22).

The entirety of Gen 6–9 is devoted to Noah's story. Despite the clear word of God given to Noah on more than one occasion, there are no recorded prayers of Noah. He was a man who responded in faith and obedience to God's word, but we cannot learn much about prayer from Noah. What we know was that Noah worshipped in response to God's word to him. After the flood had subsided and the animals came out of the ark (Gen 8:14–17), "Then Noah built an altar to the LORD and took some of every clean animal and some of every clean bird and offered burnt offerings on the altar" (Gen 8:20). Noah worshipped the LORD because he had been saved from death through the ark and he knew that God had fulfilled his word to Noah. This offering on the altar was received by God as pleasing, resulting in a promise that there would be no repeat of this great judgement on the earth (Gen 8:21–22). In this respect, Noah's offering on the altar acted as a form of intercession for all who would come after him. Noah and his offering "stand in the breach" (see Ezek 22:30) between a holy God and a world of sinners. Noah may have meant it only as a way of expressing praise for God's redemptive action, but it functioned according to God's purposes for the preservation of the world.

The Tower of Babel: A False Religious System

The flood showed us God's actions to rid the world of people who did not want to obey him and yet the flood did not rid the world of sinners. The descendants of Noah became the nations of the world. Those nations appeared to have learned nothing from the flood. Instead of worshipping the God who made heaven and earth, and who brings judgement upon sinners, they decided to embrace a false religion, one in which it is not God who takes the initiative but humans.

"And they said to one another, 'Come, let us make bricks, and burn them thoroughly.' And they had brick for stone, and bitumen for mortar. Then they said, 'Come, let us build ourselves a city and a tower with its top in the heavens, and let us make a name for ourselves, lest we be dispersed over the face of the whole earth'" (Gen 11:3–4). The people were building a ziggurat, a tower topped with a shrine or temple. The tower builders hoped to reach heaven by their own cleverness and skill. There was a design to their religious longings. They were the ones who would reach up to God and not God down to them. They were the ones who would make a name for themselves and not God who would give them such honour. They believed themselves in control of the world because of this tower to heaven. But God scattered them in order to thwart their goals (Gen 11:5–9). That city was called Babel, a name which sounds like the Hebrew for confused.

The religious system of the tower of Babel was the prototype of every false system of prayer. False systems of prayer are based on the arrogant belief that human beings can reach up to God and please him by their cleverness and industry. However, if God does not reach down to us and gift us with the possibility of prayer, there can be no genuine prayer. False religions offer prayers that are human generated. The true and living God has not made any promises about hearing the prayers prayed to false gods. False religions, praying to false gods, do not rely on God to offer grace but devise schemes to get God to do what they desire. Sadly, many such schemes are pedalled as Christian, but any form of prayer not based upon God's grace towards us is false.

Abraham: Friend of God

In total contrast to the human-centred religion of the tower of Babel, there was Abram (later Abraham). Abram was not a man who sought out God. The total opposite was true. God sought out Abram. We know that before God called him, Abram was probably an idol worshipper like his family (Josh 24:2). What changed things for Abram was that the LORD called him and made a covenant with him.

> Now the LORD said to Abram, "Go from your country and your kindred and your father's house to the land that I will show you. And I will make of you a great nation, and I will bless you and make your name great, so that you will be a blessing. I will bless those who bless you, and him who dishonours you I will curse, and in you all the families of the earth shall be blessed." So Abram went, as the LORD had told him, and Lot went with him. Abram was seventy-five years old when he departed from Haran. (Gen 12:1–4)

If we compare the builders of the tower in Gen 11 with the call of Abram in Gen 12, we find clear differences. For a start, the pronouns are telling. The tower builders said, "let us" and "lest we". The call of Abram did not contain a human word of what humans must do, but rather a divine word: "I will show you", "I will make", "I will bless" and "I will curse". God was the one whose actions defined what Abram was to do, the opposite of the story of the tower in which human actions defined what must happen. Secondly, the tower builders wanted to make a name for themselves (Gen 11:4), but for Abram it was God who would make a name for him (Gen 12:2). Thirdly, the covenant and God's blessing were not the result of Abram's cleverness but God's choice. Fourthly, Abram responded to God's call by leaving his home and family as God told him to. Henceforth, Abram was in covenant relationship with the living God, the Creator of heaven and earth.

The LORD's promises were the reason for Abram's worship. The LORD promised that Abram's offspring would possess the land and Abram built an altar and worshipped. He later built an altar and called on the name of the LORD (Gen 12:7–8). This is a way of saying that he began to pray to the true God instead of the false gods of his upbringing. We don't see any specific prayers spelled out at this point in Abram's life. There are some in later chapters. Nonetheless, the basis of his worship and prayer was the relationship that the LORD established with him (not the other way around).

Whatever Abram did was blessed by God in accordance with the promise of God given in Gen 12:2. But Abram was yet to receive the blessing of a child. In Gen 15 there was a conversation between the LORD and Abram about this very thing.

> After these things the word of the LORD came to Abram in a vision: "Fear not, Abram, I am your shield; your reward shall be very great." But Abram said, "O Lord GOD, what will you give me, for I continue childless, and the heir of my house is Eliezer of Damascus?" And Abram said, "Behold, you have given me no offspring, and a member of my household will be my heir." And behold, the word of the LORD came to him: "This man shall not be your heir; your very own son shall be your heir." And he brought him outside and said, "Look toward heaven, and number the stars, if you are able to number them." Then he said to him, "So shall your offspring be." And he believed the LORD, and he counted it to him as righteousness. (Gen 15:1–6)

By this point in his relationship with the God who called him, Abram was able, not only to offer sacrifice and praise, but to converse with God. This was, of course, a conversation that began with God's promise to Abram. Yet Abram responded with a question about how God's promise could be fulfilled in his life. God did not rebuke Abram for this question but instead offered more promises. The result was that Abram believed God and God counted Abram righteous due to his faith. This is why Abram was called "a friend of God" (2 Chr 20:7; Isa 41:8; Jas 2:23).

Abram's faith was key in his relationship with God. At that point in time there was no fulfilment of the promises. The son of promise was not born to him for probably fifteen more years after this. Yet, as Abram trusted God he could pray confidently. We can see this in the next couple of verses, in which God made another promise and Abram again asked a question as to how it would happen (Gen 15:7–8). Abram would be long dead before it this promise—namely, that his offspring would possess the land—came to pass (Gen 15:12–15). His conversation with the LORD came from a place of trust in God's word, even though that word would not be wholly fulfilled in his lifetime (compare Heb 11:13). (Note that a similar interaction between God's promises and Abram's questions appears in Gen 17, particularly verses 17–18.)

Christians have been called friends of God by Jesus (John 15:15). As friends of God, we have received from him "precious and very great promises" (2 Pet 1:4). Abram responded to the word that God spoke to him, but we should not expect God to speak to us directly in the way he spoke to Abram. While there is no doubt that God is *able* to speak this way, as a general rule, he has spoken his word and it is now written down in the Bible for our instruction. Direct words from God are rare and often the feelings we experience as words from God are nothing more than feelings, and therefore not reliable. What we can rely on are the words of Scripture. Our prayer can rightly be a response to these promises. Our confidence in prayer is that God has made a covenant with us through Christ (Luke 22:20; 1 Cor 11:25; 2 Cor 3:6).

Abram was a friend of God and yet he was not immune from making poor choices. He had the promise of God regarding a son and still he decided to take the matter of having an heir into his own hands. Abram's wife suggested a solution to the problem: Get the maid pregnant and her child can be the heir (Gen 16:1–2). Abram had a unique relationship with the living God. Yet, instead of praying for

God's wisdom and God's will on the matter, Abram simply agreed with his wife and went ahead and had sex with Hagar the maid. The birth of Ishmael, Hagar's son, would have long-lasting consequences for the Middle East. Ishmael is the father of the Arab nations, who have been in ongoing conflict with Israel. Just as Eve might have been saved from becoming the first sinner through asking God for help, Abram might have prevented the present conflict in the Middle East by praying instead of simply leaping into this faithless action.

Over time, the depth of Abram's relationship with God grew. As with the initial call to follow the LORD, his new experience of prayer was initiated by God. Just before Sarah became pregnant with Isaac, the LORD appeared to Abraham (God had changed his name in Gen 17).

> The LORD said, "Shall I hide from Abraham what I am about to do, seeing that Abraham shall surely become a great and mighty nation, and all the nations of the earth shall be blessed in him? For I have chosen him, that he may command his children and his household after him to keep the way of the LORD by doing righteousness and justice, so that the LORD may bring to Abraham what he has promised him." (Gen 18:17–19)

This word from God was the precursor to Abraham interceding for Sodom and Gomorrah. The LORD told Abraham that he would come to examine the sins of Sodom and Gomorrah (Gen 18:20–21). When Abraham heard this, he pleaded for God to spare the righteous. It is likely that he was conscious of the fact that his nephew Lot lived in Sodom with his family.

> Then Abraham drew near and said, "Will you indeed sweep away the righteous with the wicked? Suppose there are fifty righteous within the city. Will you then sweep away the

place and not spare it for the fifty righteous who are in it? Far be it from you to do such a thing, to put the righteous to death with the wicked, so that the righteous fare as the wicked! Far be that from you! Shall not the Judge of all the earth do what is just?" (Gen 18:23–25)

Abraham knew God's character. He knew that the God he worshipped is the righteous judge and will not act unjustly. Because God is just, Abraham could pray boldly for the LORD to spare the righteous living in Sodom.

The LORD responded to Abraham's plea with a promise that fifty righteous would be sufficient for him to save the cities. Hence, Abraham was bold—even knowing his frail mortality in the presence of the eternal God—and asked God to spare the city for forty-five righteous, then forty, then thirty, then twenty and finally ten. This the LORD agreed to, and he left Abraham. This interaction was only possible because God came to Abraham and told him what he would do. As a friend of God, Abraham was aware of God's intended actions and prayed about them. His intercession was not begun out of his own thoughts and desires but prompted by God's word to him. The answer to this prayer is recorded in Gen 19, when Lot and his daughters were rescued from Sodom by angels (Gen 19:29).

Jesus told us what it means to be a friend of God. "No longer do I call you servants, for the servant does not know what his master is doing; but I have called you friends, for all that I have heard from my Father I have made known to you" (John 15:15). Those who are God's friends are privy to what God is doing in the world. It is impossible in such a short space to expound upon God's purposes for the world. However, in a general sense, he desires humans to be saved and know the truth about him (1 Tim 2:4). This is part of his plan to unite all things in Christ (Eph 1:10). Knowing this, Christians can intercede for the world as Abraham interceded for Sodom and Gomorrah. We may pray that God might put off the final judgement so that many more people might come to know him (see 2 Pet 3:9).

It is interesting at this point to compare Abraham pleading for Sodom and Gomorrah and the absence of a recorded prayer of Noah. The New Testament calls Noah "a herald of righteousness" (2 Pet 2:5). God warned Noah of the coming flood and Noah obeyed God's command to build an ark (Heb 11:7). But the Bible records no scene like the one with Abraham and the LORD discussing what would happen. I can only speculate here about this lack. It is possible that God had determined to cleanse the earth and had no desire to save any but Noah and his family. Therefore, he did not prompt Noah to intercede for the righteous, because there were no righteous people on earth at that time. This seems to me to be the best explanation of the absence of such a prayer on the lips of Noah. If God had desired to spare more than Noah and his family, he would have sovereignly caused Noah to pray for the righteous. But this did not happen.

Abraham's role as an intercessor was revisited in Gen 20. Abraham and Sarah went to live in the Negev and Abraham passed off Sarah as his sister. She was put in the harem of Abimelech. So, God came to Abimelech in a dream and warned him to return Sarah to her husband or die. What is interesting is that this dream did not summon Abimelech to pray but instead told him that Abraham would pray for him. Abraham was in covenant relationship with the LORD—a covenant initiated by God—but Abimelech was not. Abraham was called a prophet (Gen 20:7), a status that flowed from that covenant relationship.

This tells us that prayer is very much dependent upon relationship with God. Unbelievers cannot expect to pray and be heard by God. But those who are called by God to pray can expect their prayers to be heard. This was true of Abraham's prayer for Abimelech. "Then Abraham prayed to God, and God healed Abimelech, and also healed his wife and female slaves so that they bore children. For the LORD had closed all the wombs of the house of Abimelech because of Sarah, Abraham's wife" (Gen 20:17–18).

The Prayer of Abraham's Servant

I will consider one final prayer in Genesis, that of Abraham's servant. Abraham sent his most senior servant back to his family—who lived in the place he originated from—in order to get a wife for the son of promise, Isaac. Abraham insisted that the servant was not to take Isaac back to that place. He was confident that God would provide a suitable wife for the servant to bring back to Canaan for Isaac (Gen 24:1–9).

The servant was also a man of faith. So, when he arrived at his destination, he prayed before continuing.

> And he said, "O LORD, God of my master Abraham, please grant me success today and show steadfast love to my master Abraham. Behold, I am standing by the spring of water, and the daughters of the men of the city are coming out to draw water. Let the young woman to whom I shall say, 'Please let down your jar that I may drink,' and who shall say, 'Drink, and I will water your camels'—let her be the one whom you have appointed for your servant Isaac. By this I shall know that you have shown steadfast love to my master." (Gen 24:12–14)

It is worth dissecting this prayer. The servant addressed God both by the name LORD and "God of my master Abraham". This man had spent many years in the house of Abraham so he would have learned about the LORD, the God whom Abraham followed, who spoke to Abraham and to whom Abraham prayed. At that point in history,

Abraham was *the* friend of God, the *one* man through whom all would be blessed (Gen 12:3). If this servant wanted his prayer answered it makes sense that he would come to God through reference to Abraham. As we saw earlier, covenant relationship with God is vital for prayer. Without this there is no reason to hope for an answered prayer. Because of the servant's association with Abraham, he would have experienced God's blessing. Since he was a servant in Abraham's household, he would have been circumcised, and thus included within the covenant with God (Gen 17:12–13). The servant recognized that he needed this covenant relationship with God through Abraham in order to find God's blessing upon his search for a bride for Isaac. Similarly, we should understand our need of Christ in order to come to God, because without Christ there is no covenant relationship with God.

The servant then asked for a sign so that he could be sure of the LORD's leading. No doubt, the servant was aware that Isaac was the miraculous child, born to Sarah in her old age. He probably also knew that God had promised that blessing would flow through Isaac and his line. Hence it was vitally important for the servant to choose the right woman as a bride. The New Testament does not teach us to seek for signs in this sense. Christian believers are all given the indwelling Holy Spirit. But there is no indication that Abraham or his servant were indwelt by the Holy Spirit. Later in the Old Testament there were means given by which a person could inquire of God—through priest or prophet. At that time, neither priestly class nor prophets (aside from Abraham himself) existed for the servant to consult. Asking for a sign, then, made good sense. In fact, God answered with exactly the requested sign (Gen 24:15–21). However, we should be careful not to expect such signs.

Conclusion

Genesis is foundational to the history of Israel because it gives context to where the nation of Israel sprung from. It began with the broad view of creation and the nations of the world, and then focused on Abraham and the patriarchs. In regard to prayer, we have seen negative and positive examples of how to pray. Cain was unwilling to ask God to help him overcome temptation. Noah alone in the earth worshipped God and the rest were wiped out. The people of Shinar sought out their own version of prayer by building a tower to heaven.

But Abraham was a good example for us with respect to faith and prayer, two things which stand together. Abraham was our example because he knew the true God. Prayer for Abraham was a response to God's word to him, offered with the confidence that comes from being placed into covenant relationship with God. The blessings of Abraham are graciously given to Christians by faith in Jesus (Gal 3:14). Consequently, an even better covenant relationship with God is given to believers because Jesus is the mediator of a better covenant (Heb 7:22). Just as Abraham was a friend of God, so too Christians can experience the confidence in prayer which Abraham had.

Reflection Questions / Journal Prompts

1. Consider whether your prayer life is based on God's grace towards you in Christ or whether you have tried to devise schemes to get God to do what you desire.
2. Jesus called his disciples friends (John 15:13–15). As a believer in Christ, what difference does it make to your prayer life that you are called a friend of God?
3. How has your prayer life grown as you have walked with God over many years?
4. Recall a time in which you have received God's clear direction

in response to prayer.

Exodus: The Prayer Life of Moses Part 1

Exodus outlines how God delivered the Israelites from Egypt and made them into a nation whose God is the LORD. Exodus provides us with a great deal of insight into the prayer life of Moses. He was the greatest leader of Israel and their greatest prophet (excluding the Lord Jesus Christ, of course). Moses went from being a man who did not know God and relied on his own wisdom, to a man called by God but scared to do what God asked, to a confident leader and intercessor for Israel.

The Israelites Cried Out to God

But before we look at Moses, there is one important prayer that sets the scene for the exodus from Egypt, and indeed the call of Moses to lead the people out. Exodus begins by recounting what happened to the family of Jacob after they moved to Egypt (following on from the account at the end of Genesis). The leadership of Egypt changed, and the new king was ignorant of Joseph and what he did for Egypt. The result was that the Israelites were made into slaves and oppressed. Even the very survival of the Israelite people was threatened (Exod 1). Moses was a Hebrew, but he was raised by Pharaoh's daughter. When he was grown, he tried to get justice for his fellow Israelites, but he made a bad choice and fled to Midian (Exod 2). It is at this point that we find the first prayer of the book.

During those many days the king of Egypt died, and the people of Israel groaned because of their slavery and cried out for help. Their cry for rescue from slavery came up to God. And God heard their groaning, and God remembered his covenant with Abraham, with Isaac, and with Jacob. (Exod 2:23–24)

A couple of aspects of this prayer deserve comment. First of all, the people groaned and cried out for help. It is not clear to what extent words were involved in this prayer. Perhaps some words were used. Perhaps the words were very few. People in pain, people who are suffering, rarely have the energy to use words. They groan and cry. Words sometimes simply won't come out. Prayer can often be like this. What matters in this case is that the prayer, wordless as it most likely was, was directed towards God in heaven. He does not need words in order to understand what we need. And he heard their groaning.

Secondly, the reason why God paid heed to their groaning is given to us. "God remembered his covenant with Abraham, with Isaac, and with Jacob." God is not arbitrary in who he hears and who he does not listen to. He hears prayer on the basis of his covenant relationship with people. In this case, the LORD was in covenant relationship with Abraham, Isaac, Jacob and their descendants. When God called Abraham he promised, "I will bless those who bless you, and him who dishonours you I will curse, and in you all the families of the earth shall be blessed" (Gen 12:3). God is faithful to his promises. The Egyptians were dishonouring Israel and God would therefore act against Egypt and for Israel on the basis of this promise. The story of the exodus (Exod 3–15) is the story of God honouring his promise to Abraham. God's covenant relationship with his people is still the basis for answered prayer. However, we are under the new covenant, the covenant initiated by the blood of Jesus (Luke 22:20; 1 Cor 11:25).

Moses Met the LORD

The remainder of this chapter will focus on the prayers of Moses in Exodus. The first time that Moses prayed was in response to the presence of God at the burning bush. Moses saw the bush and went to investigate. "God called to him out of the bush, 'Moses, Moses!' And he said, 'Here I am'" (Exod 3:4b). God chose Moses to be his spokesman as he delivered Israel from Egypt. This choice does not imply that Moses was a man of prayer prior to this event. We have no indication that Moses prayed while he was hiding in Midian. It would be wrong to assume that Moses was the driving force of the exodus. That place belongs the God who made a covenant with Abraham and who fulfils his promises because he is faithful.

As Moses stood at the burning bush, God promised him that he would deliver Israel from Egypt and take them to their own land. Each time God spoke, Moses responded to God's word to him by questioning: Who am I?; Who are you?; What shall I do if they don't believe me?; I am not eloquent. God answered each of these questions and concerns. During this God-initiated conversation, Moses grew in his understanding of the God who had called him. However, despite God's willingness to answer him, Moses asked God to send someone else. It was the final request that caused God to become angry (Exod 4:13–14). Although the questions were acceptable to God, the lack of faith Moses showed was not acceptable.

Moses and Aaron did as God said and went to Pharaoh to demand that he release the people. But Pharaoh made the Israelites work even harder (Exod 5:1–18). Then the people complained to Moses and Aaron. They did not pray directly, perhaps because they did not know God yet. But Moses prayed in response to the complaints of the people. "Then Moses turned to the LORD and said, 'O Lord, why have you done evil to this people? Why did you ever send me? For since I came to Pharaoh to speak in your name, he has done evil to this people, and you have not delivered your people at all'" (Exod 5:22–23). Despite what looks very much like unbelief in God's word to him, the LORD responded to

Moses by reiterating his promise of deliverance, based on his covenant (Exod 6:1–5). Such is the graciousness of God to his servants.

Moses Prayed for Pharaoh

Moses and Aaron went to Pharaoh again, first with a sign and then with a plague of blood to back up their request. This was followed by a plague of frogs (Exod 7:8–8:7). At this point, there was a new development in the prayer life of Moses. Pharaoh called Moses and asked him to pray to the LORD to take away the frogs. He promised that when they were gone he would let the Israelites go (Exod 8:8). As events progressed, a pattern developed of Pharaoh asking Moses to pray to the LORD on his behalf—8:28 (plague of flies), 9:28 (plague of thunder and hail), and 10:17 (plague of locusts). Each time, Moses prayed to the LORD and the plague was removed (although Pharaoh did not ever genuinely repent).

These incidents have some parallels to the intercession of Abraham for Abimelech (Gen 20:17). Pharaoh worshipped the false gods of Egypt, and he would not pray to the LORD, the God of Israel. Nor would the God of Israel respond to the prayers of a faithless man, even if he was the king of Egypt. Pharaoh shared an understanding with Moses that Moses knew his own God and therefore he should be the one to pray to his God. Prayer cannot be to a generic god, as if all gods are the same. As the apostle Paul says, "For although there may be so-called gods in heaven or on earth—as indeed there are many 'gods' and many 'lords'—yet for us there is one God, the Father, from whom are all things and for whom we exist, and one Lord, Jesus Christ, through whom are all things and through whom we exist" (1 Cor 8:5–6). Only the true and living God was responsible for the plagues and only the true and living God could cause them to cease.

From a different perspective, Moses' prayers were effective because God had chosen and elected him. This was not a position that Moses was able to acquire for himself. It was God's choice alone. There is very little said about the prayer life of the Israelites themselves. As a rule, it was Moses who spoke to the LORD on behalf of Israel, or in the above instance on behalf of Pharaoh. In terms of applying this to Christians, Moses was a type of Christ. This means that Moses, as a mediator between God and Israel, pointed forward to the Lord Jesus Christ, who is the one mediator between God and humanity (1 Tim 2:5). This is why God answered Moses' prayer for Pharaoh and why Pharaoh could not simply pray for himself. The distinction we must observe is that now Christians can pray and intercede for unbelievers and be heard through Jesus.

Moses Prayed for Israel

After the exodus, Moses' intercession was on behalf of the people of Israel. As in Egypt, the people complained to Moses and Moses took the problem to the LORD. There was no water (Exod 15:24–25) and then no food (Exod 16:3–4), and again no water to drink (Exod 17:1–4). Moses prayed and the LORD dealt with the problem. It was quite possible that instead of grumbling to Moses, the Israelites could have directed their concerns to God since he is concerned with our needs (see Matt 6:8). Christians should recognize the truth that God has granted us the status of mature sons because of Christ (Gal 4:1–7). The consequence of this is our access to God. There are not special Christians who must pray on behalf of the rest of us. In their grumbling, the people of Israel were acting like small children instead of people of God, who had a real relationship with him.

Moses interceded for Israel on several different occasions. It was Moses who interceded for Israel in the fight against the Amalekites. This was described as Moses holding up the staff of God (Exod 17:8–9). Intercession for the success of Israel's army was Moses' contribution to the battle, while Joshua led the army to victory (Exod 17:13). When the people came to Mt Sinai, Moses alone went up the mountain to God. He heard from the LORD, passed the word onto the people, and then brought the answer of the people back to God (Exod 19:3–9). Later in Exodus, Moses was called to draw near to God. Some of Israel's leaders could go part of the way, but the general population of Israel could not draw near to God (Exod 24:1–2).

These incidents should be understood through the lens of Moses as mediator, as discussed above. Moses as the only man who could come close to God is something unique to Exodus, rather than a pattern for Christian leadership as such. Christians still need a mediator but now we have the perfect mediation of Christ. Christ is the mediator of a better covenant than the covenant God made with Moses or even the Abrahamic covenant (Heb 8:6; 9:15; 12:24). This is due to the fact that Jesus is both fully human and fully God in the one person. He therefore stands on both sides of the divide. This truth is vital because it means that Christians do not need to pray through the mediation of church leaders, such as pastors. Pastors can pray with us, but we can also pray ourselves. Christian prayer is an intense privilege, as these incidents in Exodus demonstrate for us.

The final example of Moses' prayer life in Exodus spans over several chapters. Moses had been up the mountain with the LORD and received the Ten Commandments on tablets of stone, along with the law (Exod 24:15–31:18). While he was gone, the people built a golden calf, called it their god and worshipped it (Exod 32:1–6). Moses knew nothing of this until alerted by God.

> And the LORD said to Moses, "Go down, for your people, whom you brought up out of the land of Egypt, have corrupted themselves. They have turned aside quickly out of the way that I commanded them. They have made for themselves a golden calf and have worshipped it and

sacrificed to it and said, 'These are your gods, O Israel, who brought you up out of the land of Egypt!'" And the LORD said to Moses, "I have seen this people, and behold, it is a stiff-necked people. Now therefore let me alone, that my wrath may burn hot against them and I may consume them, in order that I may make a great nation of you." (Exod 32:7–10)

It was this word from the LORD which prompted Moses to intercede with God for the nation. God was truly angry with Israel because of their sin, but he could have simply obliterated them while Moses was on the mountain. He did not need to let Moses know about it. Yet, the LORD informed Moses, just as he informed Abraham about Sodom and Gomorrah in Gen 18. This is a clear indication that God led Moses to argue with him so that he might spare those who sinned against him. This is exactly what Moses did in response to God's word to him about what had happened.

But Moses implored the LORD his God and said, "O LORD, why does your wrath burn hot against your people, whom you have brought out of the land of Egypt with great power and with a mighty hand? Why should the Egyptians say, 'With evil intent did he bring them out, to kill them in the mountains and to consume them from the face of the earth'? Turn from your burning anger and relent from this disaster against your people. Remember Abraham, Isaac, and Israel, your servants, to whom you swore by your own self, and said to them, 'I will multiply your offspring as the stars of heaven, and all this land that I have promised I will give to your offspring, and they shall inherit it forever.'" (Exod 32:11–13)

In this prayer of intercession, Moses used three arguments to sway God against ending Israel as a nation. The first was a reminder of the fact that God rescued his people by his great power. His redemptive actions on behalf of Israel were a reason to not obliterate them. Why redeem them with a purpose and not fulfil that purpose? The second argument was connected to the first. The Egyptians would interpret the death of all Israel as God having rescued Israel with evil intent. It would be as if God were undecided about what to do with this people. Therefore, if he destroyed them, his glory would be undermined among the nations who saw what happened. Lastly, Moses reminded God of his promises to Abraham, Isaac and Israel. God cannot turn away from his own word and will by nature keep his promises. Moses knew this and pleaded for God to turn away from his anger. This is exactly what God did (Exod 32:14).

Moses' intercession after the golden calf incident did not end there. According to Deuteronomy, Moses also prayed for Aaron because the LORD was ready to destroy him as well as the people (Deut 9:19–20). The intercession of Moses continued further after he had spoken with Aaron and tried to deal with the peoples' sin. Moses went to God hoping to atone for the sin. He pleaded with God to forgive their dreadful sin by offering to be blotted out of God's book, an offer which God refused. There was still punishment to follow because of the sin but God did not wipe out all of Israel (Exod 32:15–35).

Moses Prayed for Himself

After this event, Moses sought to know the LORD in a more intimate way. "Moses said to the LORD, 'See, you say to me, "Bring up this people," but you have not let me know whom you will send with me. Yet you have said, "I know you by name, and you have also found favour in my sight." Now therefore, if I have found favour in your sight, please show me now your ways, that I may know you in order to find favour in your sight. Consider too that this nation is your people'" (Exod 33:12–13). This prayer for greater knowledge of God was based on what God had said to Moses in the past: "I know you by name, and you have also found favour in my sight." Although this statement is not recorded elsewhere, it is clear that Moses heard God say it in the past. Moses used this word of God as a starting point for seeking God and his ways. In this respect this prayer is like previous prayers in that it was based on God's word.

God then promised to go with Moses, and Moses asked again that God would fulfil this word, which he did (Exod 33:14–17). But then Moses went further and asked for something which God had not promised him. "Moses said, 'Please show me your glory'" (Exod 33:18). This prayer was only partially answered because the LORD is holy and his glory cannot be fully seen; anyone who sees God's face will die (Exod 33:19–20). Moses took two new stone tablets up the mountain and there the LORD passed by him, proclaiming his name, his mercy and compassion, and his holiness. This prompted Moses to plead again that God would go with Israel on the journey to the Promised Land and forgive the people (Exod 34:1–9). This demonstrates that God's revelation of his character and mercy, even his holiness, is a catalyst to prayer, to petition and intercession.

Conclusion

The prayer life of Moses matured as he got to know God more and more. In the beginning, Moses spent a lot of time complaining to God about things. As he came to experience God's word to him and see God's redemptive actions on behalf of the people, Moses grew more confident with God. He turned into a powerful intercessor. He knew the kind of God he served and could pray according to what God had said and done in the past. Moses' prayer life was always a response to God's word. This man knew that God is a God of his word. He is faithful to his promises. He upholds his own glory for the sake of his people. He is holy and righteous, yet merciful and compassionate.

We should note, however, that there are certain aspects of Moses' prayer life that we can emulate and others we cannot. It would be foolish, for example, to wait for a burning bush before entering into prayer. You and I are unlikely to ever experience something like this. Nor is it likely that we will be called to rescue thousands of people out of a nation that is enslaving them and then miraculously cross the sea on dry land. None of us can, or need to, be a mediator between God and his people. This role is for Christ alone. We can, nonetheless, imitate Moses' prayer life through prayers that reflect God's promises and character. We too can be confident that God will be faithful to his promises when we pray.

Reflection Questions / Journal Prompts

1. Describe a time when you prayed with few words in your pain. How did God answer you?
2. How has your prayer life grown over time? What has given you greater confidence in prayer?
3. How does knowing that Jesus Christ gives believers direct access to God the Father change your thinking about prayer?
4. Consider the character of God. Are your prayers focused on giving God glory? Do you pray according to the character of God? As a consequence, what needs to change in your prayers?

Numbers: The Prayer Life of Moses Part 2

The events in the book of Numbers took place after Israel had been out of Egypt for two years. The book gives us even more examples of Moses' prayer life. While there are similarities to what we read in Exodus, there are also differences. The similarities are present because the same sinful people who made up the people of Israel in Exodus appear in the stories in Numbers. Sinful people sin and need someone to intercede for them. The differences include the rebellions that some decided to stage against Moses, and the need for Moses to pray for himself.

Moses Prayed for Help

Some time had passed since the exodus. One might think that the Israelites had learned who the LORD is and what he is like because even beyond the miraculous deliverance from Egypt, he had fed them in the desert, given them water, and shown them both his holiness and mercy. However, after the people set out from Mt Sinai, "the people complained in the hearing of the LORD about their misfortunes, and when the LORD heard it, his anger was kindled, and the fire of the LORD burned among them and consumed some outlying parts of the camp" (Num 11:1). Again, Moses was forced to intercede for the people so that the fire from God would stop consuming the people. Yet, the people continued to complain about food and insisted that they wanted to go back to Egypt (Exod 11:2–6).

By this point, Moses was fed up and weary because of the continual rebelliousness of the people. He desperately needed some help and support in the enormity of his task as leader.

Moses said to the LORD, "Why have you dealt ill with your servant? And why have I not found favour in your sight, that you lay the burden of all this people on me? Did I conceive all this people? Did I give them birth, that you should say to me, 'Carry them in your bosom, as a nurse carries a nursing child,' to the land that you swore to give their fathers? Where am I to get meat to give to all this people? For they weep before me and say, 'Give us meat, that we may eat.' I am not able to carry all this people alone; the burden is too heavy for me. If you will treat me like this, kill me at once, if I find favour in your sight, that I may not see my wretchedness." (Num 11:11–15)

In his weariness, Moses brought his complaint about the people to the LORD. This prayer was not directly a response to the word of God or his promises. However, since the LORD had said previously that Moses found favour in his sight (Exod 33:12, 17), Moses was wondering what that favour looked like in practice, especially since he had the burden of thousands of complaining people. Moses simply poured out all the frustration of being unable to meet the needs of the people. There is respect—"your servant"—and desperation in this prayer. He effectively asked for God's grace towards him. The Hebrew word translated as "favour" (*ḥēn*) could just as easily be translated as "grace". The following verses tell us that God heard and answered Moses' prayer by putting the Spirit of God upon seventy elders of Israel instead of only on Moses (Num 11:16–17). We can expect, then, that prayers for help to do the will of God will be answered.

The People Rebelled

It is a good thing that Moses received help to govern the people of Israel because after this event there were a series of rebellions to deal with. First, Miriam and Aaron confronted Moses, and Miriam was afflicted with a skin disease by God. Moses prayed for her, and after seven days she was healed (Num 12). This was the most minor of the problems facing Moses.

When they came near Canaan, twelve spies were sent to explore the land. Ten brought back a bad report (Num 13). The people became hysterical and wanted to go back to Egypt and spoke about stoning Moses and Aaron. Consequently, the LORD told Moses that he would destroy Israel with a plague and make Moses into a nation in their place (Num 14:1–4, 10–12). At this point, Moses stepped up to intercede for Israel yet again.

> But Moses said to the LORD, "Then the Egyptians will hear of it, for you brought up this people in your might from among them, and they will tell the inhabitants of this land. They have heard that you, O LORD, are in the midst of this people. For you, O LORD, are seen face to face, and your cloud stands over them and you go before them, in a pillar of cloud by day and in a pillar of fire by night. Now if you kill this people as one man, then the nations who have heard your fame will say, 'It is because the LORD was not able to bring this people into the land that he swore to give to them that he has killed them in the wilderness.' And now, please let the power of the Lord be great as you have promised, saying, 'The LORD is slow to anger and abounding in steadfast love, forgiving iniquity and transgression, but he will by no means clear the guilty, visiting the iniquity of the fathers on the children, to the third and the fourth generation.' Please pardon the iniquity of this people, according to the greatness of your steadfast love, just as you have forgiven this people, from Egypt until now." (Num 14:13–19)

There were two basic arguments in this prayer of intercession: an appeal to the glory of God and an appeal to God's steadfast love (*ḥesed*). Moses argued that the Egyptians knew what God had done to rescue Israel from Egypt and they would tell this to other nations. They also knew that God was present with his people. But those who had heard of him would think that he is weak and unable to do what he promised if he killed the whole nation. In other words, killing the whole nation would result in the glory of God being blasphemed. Moses' second argument was that the LORD is righteous but forgiving of sin because of his great love for them. On the basis of the LORD's character, as it had been demonstrated this far into the journey, Moses asked for God to forgive the rebellious people.

I believe that the LORD desired Moses to intercede because he told Moses what he would do in advance. Why would God both want to destroy and not want to destroy his people? This is a matter of God's holiness and faithfulness to his word. God was rightly angry with sin and with the utter faithlessness of the people, who at this point in time had seen the great power of God to deliver them, the patience and mercy of God, and his provision for them in the desert. As a result of Moses' intercession, God forgave their sin but would not let the people who came out of Egypt enter the Promised Land because of their unbelief (Num 14:20–23; see also Ps 95:7–11). Yet, God would not let his word of promise to Abraham fall to the ground (Isa 55:11; Num 14:31). Because God is always faithful to keep his promises, he caused Moses to intercede for the nation so that some might experience the fulfilment of the promise.

In Deuteronomy, when Moses recounted this time of intercession, he said, "So I lay prostrate before the LORD for these forty days and forty nights, because the LORD had said he would destroy you" (Deut 9:25). Forty days of intercession is a long time. However, there are times when praying a short prayer is woefully insufficient. When it comes to praying for the people of God it may require years of prayer to see profound changes and repentance from sin. With regard to unsaved people, is there a time-limit to the number of years we should pray for the lost to come to Christ? It is not that the Lord himself is unwilling, because he has already proven his willingness in Christ, but intercession is still necessary.

Yet another rebellion happened after the spy incident (above). Some of the Levites and Reubenites staged a rebellion against Moses and Aaron. They wanted to be counted equal with Moses and Aaron, despite the fact that the LORD had set apart Moses and Aaron to lead. They grumbled that Moses brought the nation out of Egypt to kill them in the wilderness and to lord it over them instead of taking them to the Promised Land (Num 16:1–3, 12–14). The LORD was angry with these rebels. "And the LORD spoke to Moses and to Aaron, saying, 'Separate yourselves from among this congregation, that I may consume them in a moment.' And they fell on their faces and said, 'O God, the God of the spirits of all flesh, shall one man sin, and will you be angry with all the congregation?'" (Num 16:20–22).

Yet once more, Moses (and also Aaron this time) interceded for the people of Israel. This time he appealed to the character and justice of God. Moses expected God to deal justly with those who had sinned—in this case by bringing swift death—but he also expected the LORD to spare those who had nothing to do with the rebellion. The rebels—and only the rebels—died by the hand of God (Num 16:23–35).

You would think that the ground opening up and swallowing Korah and his family and followers (Num 16:31–33) would be sufficient reason and motivation for the people to submit to the LORD. But there were more people in rebellion against Moses and Aaron. This time a plague broke out among the people until Aaron offered incense and made atonement in the midst of the people and stopped the plague (Num 16:41, 46–50). Aaron did not intercede in the same way that Moses did. Instead, he acted like the high priest that he was and offered a sacrifice for sin. Nonetheless, this action was vital because without it who knows how many people would have died that day due to their sin. The repeated actions of Moses and Aaron to intercede for the people prevented many from dying. The LORD is holy, and sin offends him. But he is also merciful and desires intercessors to call upon that mercy so that some might be saved from wrath. For Christians that intercession must be based on the perfect sacrifice of Christ because there is no other sacrifice acceptable to God.

Moses Prayed for Wisdom

In the next three instances of prayer, Moses prayed for wisdom and help from the LORD. In the first instance, the people grumbled against God, and he sent snakes to attack them (Num 21:4–6). "And the people came to Moses and said, 'We have sinned, for we have spoken against the LORD and against you. Pray to the LORD, that he take away the serpents from us.' So Moses prayed for the people" (Num 21:7). Here "pray" has the sense of intercede on behalf of another. The answer to this prayer was that God told Moses to make a bronze snake on a pole. Anyone who looked at it would be healed of the snake bite (Num 21:8–9). This occurrence points us to the Son of Man lifted up upon the cross for the spiritual healing of humanity (John 3:14–15). This notwithstanding, Moses' prayer for help was answered with mercy.

The second problem Moses prayed about was a matter of inheritance. The land passed from father to son, but one man had died without male heirs. The daughters wanted the land to stay in the family through inheriting it themselves (Num 27:1–4). Moses was charged with interpreting the difficult parts of the law and disputes among the people (Exod 18:15–22, 26). Yet he did not presume to provide an answer to this question regarding inheritance without prayer. "Moses brought their case before the LORD" (Num 27:5). And the LORD gave a decision for him (Num 27:6–11). This is a good example for Christian leaders who want to help their congregations to make difficult decisions. Prayer is vital when we face something not specifically addressed in the Bible. God promises wisdom (Jas 1:5).

The Final Prayers of Moses

The final time that a prayer of Moses is recorded in Numbers was at the end of his life. The LORD took Moses up a mountain so that he could see the Promised Land and told Moses that he would die and not enter it. "Moses spoke to the LORD, saying, 'Let the LORD, the God of the spirits of all flesh, appoint a man over the congregation who shall go out before them and come in before them, who shall lead them out and bring them in, that the congregation of the LORD may not be as sheep that have no shepherd'" (Num 27:15–17). Knowing that he would soon die, his concern was for the people he had been leading. Thus, he asked that God would provide a leader to look after the people when he died.

The corresponding account in Deuteronomy of Moses' prayer after hearing the news is less noble but not in the space of "God, that's not fair." The first prayer of Moses recorded in Deuteronomy pertains to his imminent death. "And I pleaded with the LORD at that time, saying, 'O Lord GOD, you have only begun to show your servant your greatness and your mighty hand. For what god is there in heaven or on earth who can do such works and mighty acts as yours? Please let me go over and see the good land beyond the Jordan, that good hill country and Lebanon'" (Deut 3:23–25). Moses argued on the basis of God's greatness that he should be allowed to see more of what God can do. This is generally a good way to pray because it focuses on God's character and redemptive actions rather than on the worthiness of the person praying. To pray based on your own worthiness is not a great strategy because we know that none of us is worthy (compare Mark 1:7; Luke 15:19). However, in this case, the LORD definitively refused and told Moses not to ask again (see Deut 3:26).

Conclusion

The book of Numbers offers us insight into the prayers of a man who led the people of God through their rebellions against God in the wilderness. Because these prayers pertain to leadership, they provide a pattern of prayer for Christian leaders. Granted there are aspects of Moses' leadership which cannot be translated into a model for Christian leaders. Moses was chosen by God as the mediator between the nation of Israel and God. But Christian leaders, pastors, teachers, etc., are not mediators as such. However, if we think only in terms of how Moses brought the people to God on the journey, then this is a model for Christian leaders. On several occasions Moses prayed that the LORD would not treat the nation as their sins deserved (compare Ps 103:10). He prayed that the nation of Israel would not be destroyed, despite their constant grumbling and faithlessness. Moses also asked for God's wisdom in leading them. His final prayer was for a suitable leader because he knew how important leadership is. Each of these prayers can inform the prayers of Christian leaders.

Reflection Questions / Journal Prompts

1. If you are a Christian leader—pastor, small group leader, schoolteacher or parent—you are called to pray for those in your charge. Reflect on how you might regularly bring the needs of those you are responsible for to God.
2. Recall an example of when you prayed for help in leading others. What did God's answer look like?
3. In what ways might your intercession for others include a

concern for the glory of God and take into account the mercy
of God?

4. What situations in your life require prayer for wisdom?
Which require intercession?

Prayers of Leaders in Joshua and Judges

The prayers of those who led Israel after the death of Moses are somewhat hit and miss. Some are helpful examples to us, and some are rather poor examples of how to pray. Nonetheless, because all Scripture is inspired by God (2 Tim 3:16) and given for our instruction (1 Cor 10:11), we can benefit from exploring these prayers, even if that benefit is knowing how not to do something.

Joshua Prayed and Then Failed to Pray

In the book of Joshua, there is a positive example of prayer and a negative example. The first takes place not long after the fall of Jericho. Joshua instructed the army that all of the people (except Rahab and her family) and goods from the city of Jericho must be devoted to the LORD, that is, destroyed. The silver, gold, bronze and iron were to go into the treasury of the LORD (Josh 6:17–19). Because the people were very confident after the defeat of Jericho, only a few went to fight against the city of Ai. But the men of Ai routed them, and everyone became afraid (Josh 7:2–5). At this point, Joshua did not know what to do.

> Then Joshua tore his clothes and fell to the earth on his face before the ark of the LORD until the evening, he and the elders of Israel. And they put dust on their heads. And Joshua said, "Alas, O Lord GOD, why have you brought this people over the Jordan at all, to give us into the hands of the Amorites, to destroy us? Would that we had been content to dwell beyond the Jordan! O Lord, what can I say, when Israel has turned their backs before their enemies! For the Canaanites and all the inhabitants of the land will hear of it

and will surround us and cut off our name from the earth.
And what will you do for your great name?" (Josh 7:6–9)

Joshua came to prayer with a posture of humility, tearing his clothes and putting dust on his head, like a man in mourning. In this prayer, Joshua questioned what God was doing. Israel had seen great redemptive acts of God akin to the exodus already. The Israelites had crossed the Jordan on dry land (Josh 3), just like the earlier generation came through the Red Sea on dry land (Exod 14). They had brought down the walls of Jericho without any of the usual accoutrements of battle (Josh 6). All this was in accordance with the promises of God to Abraham. But the defeat at Ai was not. It was reasonable to ask the LORD what had stopped him from fulfilling his promises. But Joshua did not simply question. He also appealed to God's glory. If the nation God had chosen and redeemed was defeated and killed, other nations would know. This would be to the detriment of God's great name and would not bring him glory.

We might ask why Joshua did not pray before attacking Ai, but God did not rebuke him for this. The real problem was the sin of keeping some of "the devoted things". This made the people of Israel "devoted to destruction" (Josh 7:10–12). It was necessary to remove the devoted things before Israel could succeed against their enemies. The person responsible had to be punished (Josh 7:13–26). Joshua could not have figured this out without prayer.

While Joshua grasped the need to pray about Israel's defeat at Ai, a little further on in the book, there is a circumstance in which Joshua failed to pray. As a result of this lack of prayer, a situation ensued that was to have lasting consequences. The background to this event was the command of the LORD to Moses that Israel should make no covenants with the people of the land once they had entered it because the people in the land worshipped false gods (Exod 23:31–33). Joshua would have been aware of this command, both as a disciple of Moses and because he was commanded to write the law on stones as soon as they entered the land (Deut 27:2–4).

When the Gibeonites, who were inhabitants of the land, heard about the success of Joshua at Jericho and Ai, they decided their best ploy was to deceive Joshua into believing they came from far away. They brought mouldy food in worn-out sacks, wore old clothes, and asked Joshua for a treaty (Josh 9:3–6). Joshua made a cursory attempt to find out where the Gibeonites were from (Josh 9:7–13). However, he failed to pray. "So the men took some of their provisions, but did not ask counsel from the LORD. And Joshua made peace with them and made a covenant with them, to let them live, and the leaders of the congregation swore to them" (Josh 9:14–15).

The idea of deception did not seem to have entered the heads of Israel's leaders. Joshua was a fool to fail to pray for wisdom and insight in this situation. His failure to pray made it impossible to obey God's command to "devote them to complete destruction" (Deut 7:2). Once the deception was found out, the leaders of Israel could not go back on their word and thus they could not kill the Gibeonites. Instead, they made them servants for the temple (Josh 9:16–23). This, however, was not the only consequence of the failure to pray.

Just a little while later, the Gibeonites were threatened by the Amorites, and Israel was forced to defend Gibeon against them (Josh 10:1–6). Much later, during the reign of King David, something worse happened because of this treaty with the Gibeonites. Saul had decided to kill the Gibeonites, and this brought bloodguilt on Saul's family. King David allowed the Gibeonites to put to death seven of Saul's male descendants (2 Sam 21:1–14). In this horrible and unlawful (Deut 24:16; 2 Kgs 14:6; Ezek 18:4) decision, King David also acted without prayer.

This story emphasises the fact that prayer is a vital part of making decisions, particularly serious decisions. Without prayer, we may well be hoodwinked, or foolishly make a poor decision. We do not know what the consequences will be or how far the ripples will extend. By the grace of God, our prayerlessness does not come back to bite us as often as it could.

Hit and Miss Examples of Prayer in Judges

Once we get to Judges, the situation in Israel had deteriorated. Joshua died and those who came after him were ignorant of God and repeatedly did evil in the sight of God (Judg 2:10–11). Hence it is unsurprising that prayer in Judges is frequently neither sophisticated nor helpful as an example.

The most basic form of prayer occurred a few times. There is a pattern in Judges. Israel worshipped foreign gods. Then they were overtaken by foreign oppressors. Finally, they cried out to the LORD and he sent a deliverer (see Judg 3:9, 15; 4:3; 6:6, 7; 10:10). In a sense this was repentance because instead of relying on the idols that they were serving, they turned back to the living God. Only in Judg 10:10, 15 is sin mentioned. In Judges, the people's cries to God for help did not involve a complex form of prayer. There was no depth of love for God, expression of praise, or trust in his promises.

Sometimes leaders prayed in response to the LORD and his word. Gideon was one such example, although much of what was probably prayer happened when Gideon was unaware of whom he was speaking to. The angel of the LORD went to Gideon (Judg 6:11) and spoke to him. Gideon did not know who this was, although the reader is told in Judg 6:14 that it was the LORD. Gideon asked for a sign, so that he would be able to present an offering (Judg 6:17–18). Later he asked God for yet another sign (wet fleece and dry ground—Judg 6:37) and another sign after that (dry fleece and wet ground—Judg 6:39). Gideon's prayers were in response to the LORD's word to him. However, most of his conversation consisted of him trying hard to avoid the task of saving Israel. The LORD answered Gideon's prayers for signs, presumably because God is merciful and accommodates himself to our weakness.

In Judg 10:11–14, although the people had cried out to him for help, the LORD told the Israelites that he would not deliver them; they should turn to their idols for help. But they promised that God could do as he pleases with them if they were delivered (Judg 10:15). God's refusal to listen to the prayers of his people shows how abhorrent idolatry is in his sight. The fact that the LORD provided a leader to deliver Israel indicates that he is merciful to those who he has chosen as his own. Yet, this does not grant us licence to expect that God will put up with our choices to run after idols in place of him, and then pray when we are in trouble.

In answer to the people's prayer above, God granted Israel a leader—Jephthah the Gileadite. Jephthah prayed, but his prayer was questionable at best.

> Then the Spirit of the LORD was upon Jephthah, and he passed through Gilead and Manasseh and passed on to Mizpah of Gilead, and from Mizpah of Gilead he passed on to the Ammonites. And Jephthah made a vow to the LORD and said, "If you will give the Ammonites into my hand, then whatever comes out from the doors of my house to meet me when I return in peace from the Ammonites shall be the LORD's, and I will offer it up for a burnt offering." (Judg 11:29–31)

The LORD was on the side of Jephthah before he ever opened his mouth to make a vow. This was evident by the fact that "the Spirit of the LORD was upon Jephthah", something very rare in the Old Testament. He need not have made such a rash vow as he did. We later discover that the one who must be sacrificed is Jephthah's daughter, his only child (Judg 11:34–35). We cannot help but wonder what or who Jephthah expected to come out of his door when he returned home. He may have hoped for an animal, but his family should not have been a surprise. The vow thus opened Jephthah to committing the sin of child sacrifice in the fashion of a Moabite (2 Kgs 3:27) or the worshippers of Molech (Lev 18:21; 20:2–5; 2 Kgs 23:10; Jer 32:35). Which god did Jephthah think he was praying to?

The lesson from Jephthah's fateful vow is that God is not the god of quid pro quo but the God of grace. Recognise that God is faithful to rescue and deliver without something to sweeten the pot as it were. God needs nothing from us beyond trust in him and obedience to his word. Rash vows are not easy to come back from. They simply demonstrate a lack of faith in God's character and his word.

The next significant leader in Israel was Samson. Samson's parents were more prayerful than Samson himself. The angel of the LORD visited Manoah's wife and told her that she would have a child who would be a Nazirite from the womb and would begin to deliver Israel (Judg 13:2–5). She told her husband what happened. "Then Manoah prayed to the LORD and said, 'O Lord, please let the man of God whom you sent come again to us and teach us what we are to do with the child who will be born'" (Judg 13:8). The angel of the LORD appeared to the woman again, and she got Manoah. Manoah wanted instructions about bringing up the child. Manoah offered a sacrifice, which was accepted. Eventually, they realised that they had been speaking to the angel of the LORD and Manoah was scared by this (Judg 13:9–22).

Manoah's prayer and his conversation with the angel suggest his desire was to do the will of God in his life. He prayed to the LORD and spoke to the angel of the LORD without knowing who it was. Both were prayer, even if he did not know it for a while. The actions of Manoah and his wife speak loudly. They were people who asked God for his help so that they might do his will and honour him with the responsibility they had been given. This is a positive example of prayer for us. If there is a responsibility given to us, we will make the most effective response by asking God to equip and direct us in it (compare John 15:5).

Although Samson's life takes up a much greater space in the narrative than that of his parents (Judg 14–16), Samson prayed only twice. The first prayer of Samson followed his victory over one thousand Philistines, when armed with the jawbone of a donkey. "And he was very thirsty, and he called upon the LORD and said, 'You have granted this great salvation by the hand of your servant, and shall I now die of thirst and fall into the hands of the uncircumcised?'" (Judg 15:18). God gave him water out of a rock. This was not a particularly deep prayer. It was the prayer of a man dedicated to God from the womb yet concerned only with his bodily needs.

At the end of his life, Samson had been taken captive by the Philistines, his eyes had been put out, and he had been made into a slave, grinding corn in prison. The Philistines wanted Samson to entertain them in the temple of their false god Dagon. Since Samson was blind, he asked the one who led him around to lead him to the pillars holding up the temple. The place was packed with Philistines—lords and ordinary people (Judg 16:21, 25–27). Samson's final words were a plea to God to allow him revenge on the Philistines.

> Then Samson called to the LORD and said, "O Lord GOD, please remember me and please strengthen me only this once, O God, that I may be avenged on the Philistines for

my two eyes." And Samson grasped the two middle pillars on which the house rested, and he leaned his weight against them, his right hand on the one and his left hand on the other. And Samson said, "Let me die with the Philistines." Then he bowed with all his strength, and the house fell upon the lords and upon all the people who were in it. So the dead whom he killed at his death were more than those whom he had killed during his life. (Judg 16:28–30)

Samson was not a pious man with a deep relationship with God. He was rather a man with very little self-control, a womanizer and someone prone to anger. His final prayer was in keeping with the pattern of angry vengeance that characterized his life (Judg 15). But God still heard his prayer and used it to bring about a great victory over the Philistines. This unsanctified man prayed, even if his prayers were fleshly and immature. This can give us hope that God will even listen to immature prayers on occasion. However, we would do better to aim for maturity in our relationship with God.

The motto of Judges is "Everyone did what was right in his own eyes" (Judg 17:6; 21:25). It should therefore be no surprise that the final prayers of the book were idolatrous or led to foolishness. In Judg 17–18, a man named Micah built a silver idol and found himself a Levite to be his personal priest. Some Danites came to that house and asked Micah to inquire of the LORD about their journey. The priest said it would be successful (Judg 18:5–6). This was all a piece of idolatrous prayer and worship. There was no good reason to believe that God was speaking through the priest. He probably said what they wanted to hear. They were happy to consult a priest in a house somewhere instead of truly inquiring of God according to what God had laid out. The Danites stole the idol and the priest and took these to the place they had conquered. This was the beginning of the idolatrous worship system of northern Israel (Judg 18:18–31).

The final examples of prayer were in relation to a ghastly incident with a Levite and his concubine, who was raped to death (Judg 19). As a result of this atrocity, all the tribes went out to seek to right this wrong in a fit of vengeance. They asked the Benjaminites to hand over the perpetrators. But they refused and gathered their own army to fight the other tribes (Judg 20:1–17). Several times the eleven tribes "inquired of God" about who should go into battle (Judg 20:18), and should they fight some more (Judg 20:23, 27). Inquiring of God was probably done through the priest, who was able to use Urim and Thummim (Exod 28:30; Num 27:21). The LORD answered these prayers. What can definitively be said is that is better to inquire of the LORD than not.

What the men of Israel did next was to make a vow not to give any daughter in marriage to a Benjaminite (Judg 21:1). "And the people came to Bethel and sat there till evening before God, and they lifted up their voices and wept bitterly. And they said, 'O LORD, the God of Israel, why has this happened in Israel, that today there should be one tribe lacking in Israel?'" (Judg 21:2–3). There was no answer from God. It seems that the choices of the people that day, whether wise or foolish, were placed upon God in this prayer. It is not always possible to get an answer from God. Sometimes, we must accept that we have not made the best choices and those choices have consequences.

Conclusion

It is unfortunate that after Moses, the leaders of Israel did not live up to the prayer life of Moses. Joshua was a disciple of Moses, chosen as Moses' successor, and yet the record of Joshua in prayer was fifty-fifty. One time Joshua sought the LORD for wisdom and received it. Another time he failed to seek the LORD and instead acted foolishly. The judges of Israel were also mixed. Some prayed and others barely prayed. Some made foolish vows to God. Prayers in Judges were often shallow and based on the desire for help from God without love for him, or the goal of personal glory or vengeance. There was no one in either Joshua or Judges who demonstrated the growth and depth in prayer that Moses did.

Christian leaders, whether leaders in church or parachurch, must see the benefit of prayers that are deep and based upon God's word. Shallow prayer and hit-and-miss prayer lives do not result in good leadership. Seeing the consequences of the less-than-ideal prayer lives of Joshua and the judges, I hope that we are encouraged to commit to deep and regular times of prayer. This is necessary so that the body of Christ is led by men and women who know God and make godly decisions, with wisdom and insight (compare Eph 1:17).

Reflection Questions / Journal Prompts

1. Consider how to build regular prayer into your decision-making process.
2. What steps are you taking to mature your relationship with God and hence mature your prayer life?
3. Compare a time when you prayed out of a desire for vengeance and a time when you prayed because you desired to do the will of God. What were the outcomes?
4. Commit to learning about the character of God. What have you learned about God's true character that has revealed the foolishness of particular past prayers?

Prayers of Two Women

There are not many examples of women praying recorded in the Old Testament. This is likely because the characters whose prayers are recorded were leaders: judges, kings, prophets. Few women fell into this category. Nonetheless, the fact that the prayer of a woman is included is an indication that a woman is just as able to pray as a man, and God hears the prayers of women among his people.

Hannah's Prayer

In the opening chapter of 1 Samuel, we learn that Hannah was one of two wives of Elkanah. This situation might well be stressful in itself, but it was made worse by Hannah's infertility. Even worse, the other wife was able to have children and she provoked Hannah. Hannah's husband's attempts at comfort did not work (1 Sam 1:1–8). Each year they went to the tabernacle in Shiloh to offer sacrifices. One particular year Hannah's prayer was recorded.

> After they had eaten and drunk in Shiloh, Hannah rose. Now Eli the priest was sitting on the seat beside the doorpost of the temple of the LORD. She was deeply distressed and prayed to the LORD and wept bitterly. And she vowed a vow and said, "O LORD of hosts, if you will indeed look on the affliction of your servant and remember me and not forget your servant, but will give to your servant a son, then I will give him to the LORD all the days of his life, and no razor shall touch his head." (1 Sam 1:9–11)

This was the prayer of a woman who desperately wanted a child, so much so that she was willing to give that child back to God. She made a vow for herself and for the child himself, should he be born. Aside from giving back the child to the LORD, Hannah made a Nazirite vow for her (potential) son. This is the meaning of the statement "no razor shall touch his head." A Nazirite was a person fully given over to the LORD for as long as the vow lasted (Num 6). (Other people who were under a Nazirite vow include Samson—Judg 13:5, and John the Baptist—Luke 1:15).

While Hannah was praying, Eli the high priest saw that she was not making any sound but only moving her lips. He thought she was drunk and told her to stop drinking. "But Hannah answered, 'No, my lord, I am a woman troubled in spirit. I have drunk neither wine nor strong drink, but I have been pouring out my soul before the LORD. Do not regard your servant as a worthless woman, for all along I have been speaking out of my great anxiety and vexation'" (1 Sam 1:15–16). All the grief Hannah had because of her childlessness was poured out before God that day. She held nothing back, knowing that God cares about his children, women included. Her grief was so great that she could barely make words, but God hears the very groaning of his people (compare Exod 2:24; Rom 8:26).

Eli pronounced a blessing upon Hannah. "Then Eli answered, 'Go in peace, and the God of Israel grant your petition that you have made to him'" (1 Sam 1:17). Hannah had a sense of God having heard her because she was no longer sad. Hannah's family worshipped before the LORD (the reason they went to Shiloh) and then went home. Sometime later Hannah conceived and bore a son. When the boy was weaned, probably about age three, Hannah took him to Shiloh and fulfilled her vow. She told Eli that this was the answer to her prayer (1 Sam 1: 18–20, 24–28). Hannah knew that the God she worshipped was able to do what she asked. She did not make a foolish vow or do this flippantly as if God could be manipulated (see Eccl 5:4–5).

God's answer to Hannah's prayer was a pivotal moment in Israel's history, rather than a response to a formula. Therefore, it is important that we do not make this into a formula for answered prayer: be upset and pray and make a vow and God will give you what you ask for. But circumstances can drive us to despair. We then have a choice about where we take that despair. Do we go to drugs or alcohol or bitterness or some distraction, or do we take that despair to God in prayer? The latter is what Hannah did and the LORD responded. She was not following a formula but entering into a relationship with God. We don't know how many times Hannah prayed about this. We do know that the family were pious and regularly went to sacrifice in the tabernacle. They were not worshipping in order to receive something.

Additionally, we know nothing of all the other infertile women in Israel and whether they prayed and received a positive answer. I know people who cannot conceive and who have prayed and not received a positive answer. If we make this a formula, then it appears that all the Christian women who are unable to have children have failed to follow the formula correctly. Thus, the assumption that we can get what we desire from God if we follow a formula results in great hurt to those who receive God's No. The sheer sovereignty of God over what happens in our lives means that there can never be a formula for prayer.

Having dropped off her only child at the temple to live with the high priest for the rest of his childhood, Hannah then prayed a prayer exalting the LORD.

> And Hannah prayed and said, "My heart exults in the LORD; my horn is exalted in the LORD. My mouth derides my enemies, because I rejoice in your salvation. There is none holy like the LORD: for there is none besides you; there is no rock like our God. Talk no more so very proudly, let not arrogance come from your mouth; for the LORD

is a God of knowledge, and by him actions are weighed. The bows of the mighty are broken, but the feeble bind on strength. Those who were full have hired themselves out for bread, but those who were hungry have ceased to hunger. The barren has borne seven, but she who has many children is forlorn. The LORD kills and brings to life; he brings down to Sheol and raises up. The LORD makes poor and makes rich; he brings low and he exalts. He raises up the poor from the dust; he lifts the needy from the ash heap to make them sit with princes and inherit a seat of honour. For the pillars of the earth are the LORD's, and on them he has set the world. He will guard the feet of his faithful ones, but the wicked shall be cut off in darkness, for not by might shall a man prevail. The adversaries of the LORD shall be broken to pieces; against them he will thunder in heaven. The LORD will judge the ends of the earth; he will give strength to his king and exalt the horn of his anointed." (1 Sam 2:1–10)

This was an inspired prayer, very similar to the psalms of David. In this Hannah never specifically speaks of her son but rather exalts the LORD for his salvation and holiness. The LORD turns the expected upside down. The mighty warrior is weak and the weak become strong. The rich are hungry and the hungry fed. The needy are exalted to sit with princes. The infertile have more children than the fertile. The LORD will judge all. Hannah's praise extended to all the LORD's works, not simply to the gift of her son. This was a profoundly kingdom prayer, which looked forward to the kingdom of God. It demonstrated that Hannah had a heart for worship of God, not merely a desire to have a child.

This desire to worship God was evident also in the fact that Hannah continued to go to Shiloh to offer sacrifice every year (1 Sam 2:19).

Hannah did not give up worshipping the LORD simply because she had received what she wanted. She wanted to please God in her life. This desire was ongoing. As Hannah honoured the LORD in fulfilling her vow and her regular worship, the LORD blessed her with further children of her own (1 Sam 2:20–21).

Esther's Prayer

The book of Esther is the story of a young Israelite girl in exile in Persia. Esther was made queen in place of the previous queen, who the king banished (Esth 1:1–2:18). While she was living in the king's palace, a noble named Haman sought to exterminate all the Jews under the reign of King Xerxes. Esther was asked to help by her uncle Mordecai. But Esther knew, queen or not, that she could not come into the king's presence without an invitation. He was just as likely to execute her as do her a favour. Esther agreed to seek the king's favour, but not without some backing from God (Esth 3–4).

Esther is an unusual book of the Bible in that it never mentions God or prayer directly. However, the assumption that God is sovereign over the lives of his people is woven throughout the book. Mordecai's statement is evidence of this. "For if you keep silent at this time, relief and deliverance will rise for the Jews from another place, but you and your father's house will perish. And who knows whether you have not come to the kingdom for such a time as this?" (Esth 4:14). Hence Esther asked Mordecai, "Go, gather all the Jews to be found in Susa, and hold a fast on my behalf, and do not eat or drink for three days, night or day. I and my young women will also fast as you do. Then I will go to the king, though it is against the law, and if I perish, I perish" (Esth 4:16).

A fast is likely shorthand for fasting and prayer. We have no details of what Esther, or the rest of the Jews, prayed. But they knew that their very lives depended on God answering this prayer. They were experiencing the consequences of living under the rule of a foreign power, indeed a foreign power which had conquered the great power of Babylon (see Dan 5). Adding the fast to prayer suggests a seriousness and desperation for God to act on their behalf. And God did answer this prayer, giving the Jews opportunity to defend themselves. This was the origin of the Jewish festival of Purim (Esth 8:15–9:32).

Did God answer this prayer because the people were desperate? Is desperation the key to getting an answer from God? Again, I would not offer such a formula for prayer. Although the book of Esther never states this, the foundational reason for God answering this prayer was his promises regarding Israel. God promised Abraham, "I will surely bless you, and I will surely multiply your offspring as the stars of heaven and as the sand that is on the seashore. And your offspring shall possess the gate of his enemies" (Gen 22:17). The promise pertains to the *nation* of Israel. Of course, individual Jews can be defeated and die. But the people as a whole cannot be wiped out because God has purposes for them. Yet prayer is still necessary in order that those purposes will be fulfilled.

Conclusion

There are some things in common between these two women. Most significantly for this study of prayer is that they were both in untenable situations and needed God to answer. They both had faith that the God of Israel hears his people. They were also prepared to sacrifice a great deal in order to see God's answer to their prayer. The answers to both prayers had enormous significance in the history of Israel. Samuel became a great leader, and the Jewish people were not wiped out.

If we seek to imitate the prayers of these two women, we can do so in a way that parallels their faith. To pray like Hannah and Esther, we must accept that God is sovereign and is the God who keeps his promises. He is worthy of our trust and worthy of praise. Secondly, God's purposes in answering prayer are regularly about his big picture. Faith accepts that the individual circumstances of our lives are not necessarily the focus of answered prayer. The circumstances of our lives may change when God answers prayer but if they do so it is because God has a greater kingdom purpose in answering us. Thus, our focus in prayer needs to widen beyond just the immediate needs of our daily existence.

Reflection Questions / Journal Prompts

1. Are you guilty of searching for a formula for answered prayer? Ask the Father in heaven for forgiveness and thank him that Jesus Christ gives us access to God (Eph 2:18).
2. What impossible situations do you need to bring to God in prayer?
3. In what ways is the sovereignty of God a comfort to you? How do your prayers reflect this?

Prayers of Samuel and Saul

S amuel and Saul were both leaders of Israel, but they were very different men. One was a godly man, who trusted in the God of Israel and obeyed him. The other was an opportunistic man, who was concerned with his own advancement and glory rather than obedience to God. Their prayers reflect the difference in their relationships with God.

Prayers of Samuel

Samuel's very existence was due to the prayer of his mother (see above). God chose him to lead Israel. Samuel's first recorded prayer took place when he was a small child living in the tabernacle with Eli, the high priest. "Now the boy Samuel was ministering to the LORD in the presence of Eli. And the word of the LORD was rare in those days; there was no frequent vision" (1 Sam 3:1). Although it was unusual to hear from the LORD, the LORD called to Samuel in the night while he was sleeping. Samuel had no idea who was calling him and had to be instructed by Eli (1 Sam 3:1–9). Samuel's prayer was brief and in response to God's call to him: "Speak, for your servant hears" (1 Sam 3:10c). The LORD then spoke to Samuel, giving him a prophetic word for Eli (1 Sam 3:11–14).

Let's not mistake Samuel's prayer as a guide to how to hear from God. That is not what was happening here. The prayer of Samuel was simply an acknowledgement that the LORD had already spoken to him. The initiative lay with God, and God had already decided to speak to Samuel long before Samuel prayed. Since as Christians, we have been given God's word in the Bible, the word of the LORD is not rare anymore. What is rare is a right response to the word of God. It is only a famine of the word of God when Christians refuse to read the Bible or pastors refuse to carefully exegete and teach it. What Samuel's prayer is a good model of is the attitude of humility before God that enables us to read the Bible (or listen to sermons) and respond to what God has said.

After Samuel grew up, he became a prophetic leader in Israel (1 Sam 3:19–21). When the Israelites went to battle with the Philistines, they were losing. Hence, they decided to bring the ark of the covenant to the battle. But the ark was captured, and Israel was soundly defeated (1 Sam 4:1–11). Ultimately, the Philistines sent the ark back (1 Sam 6). Samuel led the people of Israel in their response to the return of the ark. He called upon the people to rid themselves of their foreign gods (1 Sam 7:2b–4).

> Then Samuel said, "Gather all Israel at Mizpah, and I will pray to the LORD for you." So they gathered at Mizpah and drew water and poured it out before the LORD and fasted on that day and said there, "We have sinned against the LORD." And Samuel judged the people of Israel at Mizpah. Now when the Philistines heard that the people of Israel had gathered at Mizpah, the lords of the Philistines went up against Israel. And when the people of Israel heard of it, they were afraid of the Philistines. And the people of Israel said to Samuel, "Do not cease to cry out to the LORD our God for us, that he may save us from the hand of the Philistines." So Samuel took a nursing lamb and offered it as a whole burnt offering to the LORD. And Samuel cried out to the LORD for Israel, and the LORD answered him. (1 Sam 7:5–9)

There are various ways in which prayer occurred in this passage. Firstly, Samuel prayed for Israel. At this time, Samuel was the leader of Israel and thus had the privilege of praying for the nation. The leaders of

A BIBLICAL PATTERN OF PRAYER: EXPLORING PRAYER IN THE OLD TESTAMENT

Israel exercised a mediatorial role under the old covenant, a role which points to the sole mediation of Christ under the new covenant. The people were involved to some degree. In drawing water and pouring it out before the LORD, they offered a sacrifice to God. They fasted in contrition and confessed their sins: "We have sinned against the LORD."

But, when the people were afraid of the Philistines, they asked Samuel to pray for them so that God would save them from the Philistines. They did not pray for themselves. Hannah's prayer (above) is evidence that individual Israelites could pray. Yet these individuals did not. Perhaps because of Samuel's relationship with God as a prophet, they relied upon his prayers. Perhaps they were afraid to pray for themselves. Possibly, the people of Israel had little relationship with God and did not know how to pray. This might be why they foolishly thought that taking a golden box into battle would guarantee their victory. The ark of God was sacred, but it did not contain God, who cannot be contained.

Samuel offered a lamb and cried out for Israel, and God answered. The sacrifices were part of the intercession. Because Samuel was a priest and a prophet, he could offer sacrifices, whereas other people were not qualified to do so. We have no need of blood sacrifices now because Jesus has sacrificed himself for us (e.g., Heb 9:15). He is our only sacrifice and the ultimate intercessor, but that does not mean that we have no need to pray ourselves. In the present, Christians cannot come to God in their own qualifications because they don't have any. It is either come through Jesus or don't come.

Prayer is not exclusively the task of Christian leaders. However, it is right and good for Christian leaders to pray for the flock of God. It is also right for Christian leaders to lead those in their congregations to repentance. Along with this it is important to teach people that they can have relationship with God and also pray. Centring teaching on Christ will give Christians confidence in approaching God the Father. In this way believers will be less dependent on Christian leaders to pray instead of them, rather than with them.

When Samuel was old, the people asked for a king. "But the thing displeased Samuel when they said, 'Give us a king to judge us.' And Samuel prayed to the LORD" (1 Sam 8:6). Samuel took his concern to God, which is exactly the right person to take it to. What good would it have done Samuel to complain about this turn of events to his best friend? Only God could answer this complaint. Samuel had a relationship with God that meant he prayed when he was concerned about things which impacted his leadership of Israel. The LORD spoke to Samuel about this issue and God was not pleased either (1 Sam 8:7–8).

This prayer of Samuel's is a good example for us all when we are deeply concerned about something going on in the body of Christ. Where should our first port of call be to deal with the problem? Prayer to God is vital because problems of this magnitude cannot be solved by chats with others. It is not a bad thing to involve others in your prayer about these matters if those others recognize the problem for what it is. But Samuel turned first (if not solely) to the LORD with his concern. We must take care, though, not to continually expect direct words from the LORD in response. I do not reject such a thing outright, but it is more realistic to go to the Bible and to ask the Holy Spirit for wisdom in understanding the problem through God's written word than to expect a direct word of God.

The LORD gave Israel a king—Saul. After Saul had been appointed king, Samuel made a farewell speech in which he defended his own ministry, rebuked Israel—using lessons from their history—and warned them to obey the LORD (1 Sam 12:1–15).

"Now therefore stand still and see this great thing that the LORD will do before your eyes. Is it not wheat harvest today? I will call upon the LORD, that he may send thunder and rain. And you shall know and see that your wickedness is great, which you have done in the sight of the LORD, in asking for yourselves a king." So Samuel called upon the LORD, and the LORD sent thunder and rain that day, and all the people greatly feared the LORD and Samuel. And all the people said to Samuel, "Pray for your servants to the LORD your God, that we may not die, for we have added to all our sins this evil, to ask for ourselves a king." And Samuel said to the people, "Do not be afraid; you have done all this evil. Yet do not turn aside from following the LORD, but serve the LORD with all your heart. And do not turn aside after empty things that cannot profit or deliver, for they are empty. For the LORD will not forsake his people, for his great name's sake, because it has pleased the LORD to make you a people for himself. Moreover, as for me, far be it from me that I should sin against the LORD by ceasing to pray for you, and I will instruct you in the good and the right way. Only fear the LORD and serve him faithfully with all your heart. For consider what great things he has done for you. But if you still do wickedly, you shall be swept away, both you and your king." (1 Sam 12:16–25)

Because of the people's rebellion against God in asking for a king, Samuel prayed for thunder and rain during wheat harvest, a time when there is rarely any rain. God heard Samuel because Samuel was a prophet and because the LORD was also unhappy about the people's rebellion. This demonstration of the power of God was a mild version of what Elijah would do on Mt Carmel over two hundred years in the future (1 Kgs 18). The result of this answer to prayer was fear of God, which was totally appropriate, and fear of Samuel. The people wanted Samuel to pray for them because they were afraid that they were about to die. This episode suggests that the people had little relationship with the living God themselves. They were afraid because God is powerful, but they did not love him and his word. This is why they needed to rely on the prophet to pray on their behalf.

Samuel knew that his job was to pray for the people, but also to teach them about God so that they would be obedient to the LORD. Samuel was both prophet and priest, and both instructed God's people in the word of God (Lev 10:10–11; 2 Kgs 17:13; 2 Kgs 17:27; 2 Chr 35:3). He called the people to repentance and reminded them that the LORD would not forsake them because they were the people of God. God's election of the nation of Israel was the basis of Samuel's ongoing prayer for Israel. God instructs us in his plan for his people so that we might pray according to his will for the church. For this it is necessary to know what the Bible teaches about the purposes and plans of God. Most centrally, the purposes of God have been "set forth in Christ as a plan for the fullness of time, to unite all things in him, things in heaven and things on earth" (Eph 1:9b–10). Biblical instruction leads to biblical prayer, something which God directs so that his purposes will be fulfilled.

Prayers of Saul

Saul was the first king of Israel, chosen by God to satisfy the people's desire to have a king like the nations around them (1 Sam 8:5). As such, he was more significant in stature than in character (1 Sam 9:2). This was reflected in the way Saul related to God's instructions through Samuel. Saul was a military hero (1 Sam 11), but not obedient to God. The prelude to Saul's first attempt at prayer was the fact that his son Jonathon had attacked the Philistines. Saul wanted some direction from God about the battle.

> He waited seven days, the time appointed by Samuel. But Samuel did not come to Gilgal, and the people were scattering from him. So Saul said, "Bring the burnt offering here to me, and the peace offerings." And he offered the burnt offering. As soon as he had finished offering the burnt offering, behold, Samuel came. And Saul went out to meet him and greet him. Samuel said, "What have you done?" And Saul said, "When I saw that the people were scattering from me, and that you did not come within the days appointed, and that the Philistines had mustered at Michmash, I said, 'Now the Philistines will come down against me at Gilgal, and I have not sought the favour of the LORD.' So I forced myself, and offered the burnt offering." (1 Sam 13:8–12)

It was not Saul's place to offer sacrifice because he was a king and not a priest. In this respect, his offering was a desperate attempt to get God's favour but through illegitimate means. Saul was rebuked by Samuel. Obedience was what God required of Saul, but Saul was more concerned with his own fake piety than patient obedience to God's command. Because of this hasty action, Saul lost the kingdom that God had given him (1 Sam 13:13–14). Although offering sacrifice is not prayer, it was a means of worship if offered correctly. So, Saul was a man willing to bypass God's order for worship in order to get what he wanted. God was not pleased. Prayer, like worship, must be offered in a way that is pleasing to God.

Saul did not learn from his failure. A while later, Saul was again engaged in a battle with the Philistines.

> Then Saul said, "Let us go down after the Philistines by night and plunder them until the morning light; let us not leave a man of them." And they said, "Do whatever seems

good to you." But the priest said, "Let us draw near to God here." And Saul inquired of God, "Shall I go down after the Philistines? Will you give them into the hand of Israel?" But he did not answer him that day. (1 Sam 14:36–37).

It was not Saul's idea to inquire of God but even when he did so (through the priest), God did not answer him. Saul then assumed that it was because someone had sinned (1 Sam 14:38–39).

Earlier that day, Saul had made a foolish and hasty vow. "And the men of Israel had been hard pressed that day, so Saul had laid an oath on the people, saying, 'Cursed be the man who eats food until it is evening and I am avenged on my enemies.' So none of the people had tasted food" (1 Sam 14:24). The hasty vow had very negative consequences. For one, the men were so hungry by the end of the day that they ate meat from the plunder with the blood still in it (1 Sam 14:31–33) contrary to God's law (Lev 7:26; Deut 12:16). Secondly, Saul's son Jonathon was unaware of the vow and ate honey from the ground (1 Sam 14:25–30).

Saul asked the LORD why he did not answer. Lots were drawn and Jonathon was discovered to be the culprit. The soldiers had to convince Saul not to kill Jonathon. They argued that Jonathon was responsible for the great victory, with God's help. Saul relented and did not kill him (1 Sam 14:41–45). Saul was a man given to reckless decisions. His prayer to have someone to blame was not wise.

Sadly, this was not the only time God did not answer Saul. The next time around, Saul did something even more foolish. After Samuel had died, Saul wanted to ask God for help with the Philistines.

When Saul saw the army of the Philistines, he was afraid, and his heart trembled greatly. And when Saul inquired of the LORD, the LORD did not answer him, either by dreams, or by Urim, or by prophets. Then Saul said to his

servants, "Seek out for me a woman who is a medium, that
I may go to her and inquire of her." And his servants said to
him, "Behold, there is a medium at En-dor." (1 Sam 28:5–7)

God did not answer Saul because he had rejected Saul as king (1 Sam
15:23, 26; 16:1). There was no favour for Saul. Saul had a few means
available for getting answers from God: "dreams, Urim and prophets".
God did not speak directly to anyone except prophets. Having tried all
legitimate options, without an answer, Saul remained without genuine
repentance from sin. Instead of accepting the fact that God would not
answer him or help him, Saul decided to get guidance from Samuel
by using a medium. Consulting a medium was a great sin (Lev 20:27;
Deut 18:11). The medium succeeded in calling up Samuel, who then
told Saul again that God had departed from him and had made him an
enemy (1 Sam 28:8–16). Effectively, Saul tried to bypass God and went
to dead Samuel for guidance. This was a terribly wrong means of prayer.

Outside of God's grace towards us in Christ, there is no valid way
of getting prayer answered. We cannot turn to some other means.
Mediums, spiritists and necromancers are forbidden. Equally, other
magical means to get God's guidance or favour or answer are
unacceptable to God. These dishonour the God who created all things.
They imply that we can have power over God. Christians are not to do
these things. There is a means by which God has appointed us access
to his throne of grace so that he will hear our prayers, that is, through
Christ (Eph 2:18). Those who attempt to pray via other means will
not be accepted. There are many false teachers offering such alternative
means of getting God's favour. Secrets to answered prayer are generally
means that God has not ordained. These amount to nothing.

Does this mean that those who use these means in an attempt to get
prayer answered are not Christians? Not necessarily. Some might
merely be ignorant Christians, in need of correction. But it is also

possible that those who do these things are not believers but rather people who have not heard the gospel in its proper form and therefore do not know Christ.

Conclusion

The difference between the prayers of Samuel and the prayers of Saul seems to come down to right relationship with God. Samuel understood that he was called by God and lived obediently within that calling. He heard the word of God and did it. Saul, on the other hand, was chosen by God as king, but was disobedient. He was not patient but hasty and foolish. He had no regard for God's order in worship. Nor did he care about the law of God, something he should have known well because this was a requirement of kingship (Deut 17:18–20; 1 Sam 10:25). Saul did not understand prayer as part of a relationship with God, but more of a convenience so he could get what he wanted at the time.

Reflection Questions / Journal Prompts

1. In what ways are you seeking to grow in your relationship with God so that you can be more confident in prayer?
2. Give thanks to Father, Son and Holy Spirit for the sacrifice of Christ and access to God as a result.
3. In what circumstances are you tempted to look for shortcuts and secrets in prayer? Which Bible passages are most encouraging when this temptation arises?
4. What steps can you take to avoid making a hasty vow?

Prayers of David in 1 and 2 Samuel

David was a man of prayer. Although the largest collection of David's prayers is found in Psalms (fifty-four Psalms are labelled "A Psalm of David"), several of his prayers are recorded in 1 and 2 Samuel. Even without the Psalms, we can learn much about David's prayer life from 1 and 2 Samuel. David was always eager to inquire of God. However, his prayers became deeper as he became more settled as king.

David Inquired of the LORD

David was anointed as king and given the Holy Spirit (1 Sam 16:1–15), but it was a long time before David would effectively reign over Israel. David entered into Saul's service (1 Sam 16:14–23) and killed Goliath (1 Sam 17). He became successful in battle and the more successful David became the more Saul became jealous, angry and irrational in regard to David (1 Sam 18). Finally, Saul tried to kill David (1 Sam 19), thus beginning a long time in which he pursued David with the intent to kill him (1 Sam 20–30). During this time, David had to choose how he would relate to Saul, and how he would honour God.

David made a habit of inquiring of the LORD when he needed to make important decisions. When David first ran from Saul, he went to Ahimelech the priest at Nob and asked for provisions for himself and his men. One of Saul's men was there that day, and this is how Saul found out where David was (1 Sam 21:1–7).

Then answered Doeg the Edomite, who stood by the servants of Saul, "I saw the son of Jesse coming to Nob, to Ahimelech the son of Ahitub, and *he inquired of the LORD for him* and gave him provisions and gave him the sword of Goliath the Philistine." Then the king sent to summon Ahimelech the priest, the son of Ahitub, and all his father's house, the priests who were at Nob, and all of them came to the king. And Saul said, "Hear now, son of Ahitub." And he answered, "Here I am, my lord." And Saul said to him, "Why have you conspired against me, you and the son of Jesse, in that you have given him bread and a sword and *have inquired of God for him*, so that he has risen against me, to lie in wait, as at this day?" Then Ahimelech answered the king, "And who among all your servants is so faithful as David, who is the king's son-in-law, and captain over your bodyguard, and honoured in your house? *Is today the first time that I have inquired of God for him*? No! Let not the king impute anything to his servant or to all the house of my father, for your servant has known nothing of all this, much or little." (1 Sam 22:9–15; italics mine)

This story demonstrates that even before David ran from Saul, he was in the habit of making decisions by inquiring of God through the priest. Note that the priest was not a prophet, but instead used the Urim and Thummim (Exod 28:30), possibly a system of lots or maybe jewels that lit up, to find answers from God. The priest had no reason to assume anything was different on the day that David arrived because visiting the priest there was customary for David. Long before he became the king who wrote the great prayers of the Psalms, David sought the LORD.

Saul had Ahimelech killed, but his son Abiathar escaped and joined David (1 Sam 22:20). He would later help David inquire of the LORD. When David found out that the Philistines were attacking Keilah, he inquired of the LORD and the LORD answered him. He inquired a second time about this, and God answered again. David had a great victory at Keilah (1 Sam 23:1–5). Verse 6 spells out how David could inquire of the LORD. "When Abiathar the son of Ahimelech had fled to David to Keilah, he had come down with an ephod in his hand" (1 Sam 23:6). The ephod was a priestly garment, which would have housed the Urim and Thummim.

At that time, Saul discovered that David was in Keilah, and Saul went after him. "David knew that Saul was plotting harm against him. And he said to Abiathar the priest, 'Bring the ephod here'" (1 Sam 23:9). This was a shorthand way of asking Abiathar to inquire of God. This David did several times (1 Sam 23:10–12) and David used what God told him to escape Saul's pursuit of him and his men.

David's men kept their wives at Ziklag, but the town was attacked, and the wives and children captured. True to form, David sought God for a way of dealing with this tragedy. "And David said to Abiathar the priest, the son of Ahimelech, 'Bring me the ephod.' So Abiathar brought the ephod to David. And David inquired of the LORD, 'Shall I pursue after this band? Shall I overtake them?' He answered him, 'Pursue, for you shall surely overtake and shall surely rescue'" (1 Sam 30:7–8).

After Saul died, the pattern of inquiring of the LORD continued. David inquired of God as to where he should go. God responded that he should go to Hebron, so David took his two wives there along with his soldiers and household (2 Sam 2:1–3). He began his kingship proper with God's guidance. His desire was to honour God rather than to make himself great.

David became king over all Israel, took the city of the Jebusites and then the Philistines came set to attack. So, David inquired of the LORD again as to whether he should attack the Philistines, and the LORD told him he would defeat them (2 Sam 5:19). The Philistines were a problem yet again and David inquired of God. This time the

LORD provided David with a battle strategy; the LORD was on David's side in battle. David did what God told him to do and defeated the Philistines "from Geba to Gezer" (2 Sam 5:22–25).

Each of these times of inquiring of the LORD were inquiries about battles. This is not surprising since David was a great warrior and much of his life was spent defending against the Philistines, beginning with his battle against Goliath. He had no time to think about other things during this time. What is important from the perspective of thinking about prayer is that David did not make decisions about battles without asking the LORD what was right. Even though he was a good soldier, having practised while defending his sheep as a boy (1 Sam 17:34–36), he knew that he would do well to have the LORD on his side.

There was a certain amount of privilege given to David as God's anointed. This kind of prayer was dependent on having a priest available. David did not receive an inner response from the Holy Spirit, but God would give guidance via the priest, using the Urim and Thummim. David also received guidance from the prophet Gad at least once (1 Sam 22:5) Ordinary people would not have had these things available at all times as David did. Some might have been able to ask the priest when they were near the tabernacle, but that would have been rare. Nonetheless, the times when David inquired of the LORD were not particularly like Christian prayer. The means of inquiry was mechanical and the answers informative. But this was not a conversation with God. Christians are indwelt by the Holy Spirit and hence we have the chance for a deep relationship with God. Prayer for us is so much more than simply asking God for whether or not we should go into battle. Christian prayer is an intense privilege.

David's Prayers Matured

Later on, when David was more established as king, when he had taken Jerusalem from the Jebusites and had built his palace and was at rest from war (2 Sam 7:1), then David's prayers became different. David decided that it was wrong that the ark of God was in a tent when David was living in a palace. He wanted to build a temple. The prophet Nathan brought a message to David. David wanted to build the LORD a house, but instead the LORD would build David's house, that is, a dynasty and a kingdom forever (2 Sam 7:4–17). David responded with a great prayer.

> Then King David went in and sat before the LORD and said, "Who am I, O Lord GOD, and what is my house, that you have brought me thus far? And yet this was a small thing in your eyes, O Lord GOD. You have spoken also of your servant's house for a great while to come, and this is instruction for mankind, O Lord GOD! And what more can David say to you? For you know your servant, O Lord GOD! Because of your promise, and according to your own heart, you have brought about all this greatness, to make your servant know it. Therefore you are great, O LORD God. For there is none like you, and there is no God besides you, according to all that we have heard with our ears. And who is like your people Israel, the one nation on earth whom God went to redeem to be his people, making himself a name and doing for them great and awesome things by driving out before your people, whom you redeemed for yourself from Egypt, a nation and its gods? And you established for yourself your people Israel to be your people forever. And you, O LORD, became their God. And now, O LORD God, confirm forever the word that you have spoken concerning your servant and concerning his house, and do as

you have spoken. And your name will be magnified forever, saying, 'The LORD of hosts is God over Israel,' and the house of your servant David will be established before you. For you, O LORD of hosts, the God of Israel, have made this revelation to your servant, saying, 'I will build you a house.' Therefore your servant has found courage to pray this prayer to you. And now, O Lord GOD, you are God, and your words are true, and you have promised this good thing to your servant. Now therefore may it please you to bless the house of your servant, so that it may continue forever before you. For you, O Lord GOD, have spoken, and with your blessing shall the house of your servant be blessed forever." (2 Sam 7:18–29)

This prayer was not like all the other times David inquired of the LORD for direction. This was not simply an inquiry through the priest but rather a prayer of praise and petition. First of all, there was humility and praise for what God had done in making David king. David knew how great God is and how small he was. He did not imagine that he had become a king and had this success without the LORD. God's promises about David's future elicited praise. The prayer then went on to praise God for what he had done for Israel. God is great because he rescued Israel from Egypt, thus making his name great. He made Israel his people and himself their God. These aspects of the prayer are similar to prayers examined earlier. The foundation of the prayer was what God had done in the past. Before there was any petition there was rehearsal of God's goodness and the history of his redeeming activities for his people.

The final part of the prayer involved petition based on the promises of God. Here, David asked for God to do what he had promised to David. David's petition reiterates what God had promised to him and adds the fact that God would be glorified in bringing about his word.

The promises of God were what gave David courage to ask for these things. He praised God for the truth of God's word and, on these bases, asked for God to bless the house of David and implored the LORD to let it continue forever. Christians pray because God has spoken and given promises to us through Jesus Christ. This prayer, with its praise and reliance on God's truthfulness is a good model for us.

The glories of this prayer reverberated in David's life for some time. He was victorious in battle and compassionate towards Saul's grandson (2 Sam 8–10). But sadly, this changed when David stayed in Jerusalem instead of going with the troops to battle. While he was on the roof, he saw a woman bathing and lusted after her. This led to pregnancy and then the murder of her husband when he would not sleep with his wife while home from the battle (2 Sam 11). David might have imagined that he had gotten away with things, but God sent the prophet Nathan to rebuke him. There were to be consequences in David's life because of his sin, one of which was that the child born to Bathsheba would die (2 Sam 12:1–14).

> David therefore sought God on behalf of the child. And David fasted and went in and lay all night on the ground. And the elders of his house stood beside him, to raise him from the ground, but he would not, nor did he eat food with them. On the seventh day the child died. And the servants of David were afraid to tell him that the child was dead, for they said, "Behold, while the child was yet alive, we spoke to him, and he did not listen to us. How then can we say to him the child is dead? He may do himself some harm." (2 Sam 12:16–18)

David's response to the child's illness was to seek God through prayer and fasting. He did not eat or get off the ground for seven days. Still the child died. This was, after all, what God said would happen. There was a difference between God saying to Moses that he would wipe out Israel and then relenting when Moses prayed, and God saying that the child would die and not relenting when David prayed. God incited Moses to pray for Israel because his promises and his covenant prevented him from destroying the nation of Israel. Some individuals still died because of the sins that the people committed at the time, but the nation lived on. In the case of David, David did not pray because God desired his child to live, but because David himself desired his child to live and thought perhaps God would be merciful. However, the promise which God gave to David about a dynasty was not threatened by the death of one child.

Sometimes, despite concerted prayer, God does not relent from what he has chosen to do, and someone dies. Not every failure to heal someone is about punishment for sin. It would be wrong, not to mention hurtful, to assume that if someone dies, particularly a child, that God must necessarily be punishing sin. But nonetheless there are times when we pray and pray and plead and yet the answer is No. It is very hard when this happens. The sorrow is great. What are we to do when this happens? What David did might serve as a possible example for us.

"Then David arose from the earth and washed and anointed himself and changed his clothes. And he went into the house of the LORD and worshipped. He then went to his own house. And when he asked, they set food before him, and he ate" (2 Sam 12:20). The attendants were wondering why he did this. David's response was that it was too late. He thought the LORD might be gracious and heal the child, but he did not, so David stopped fasting and praying (2 Sam 12:21–23). David had neglected himself and his personal hygiene all the time the child was sick. This was not surprising. But then, he began to return to life. After washing, he went to the tabernacle and worshipped God. Worship of God is always appropriate. It reminds us of who he is, that he continues to be God regardless of whether he has answered prayer or not. This act of worship was a reset of David's devotion to God in the midst of his grief. Finally, David comforted his wife, and they conceived another child (2 Sam 12:24). This was part of movement into the future, a future in which God would fulfil the promises he made to David. One unanswered prayer is not the end of God's word and work in our lives.

David's Later Prayers and One Failure

For several chapters there are no recorded prayers of David after his sin with Bathsheba, even as his sons ran amok (although some psalms record what happened during this time). However, this was not the end of David's prayers in Samuel. While Absalom was conspiring to take over as king, David had to flee for his life (2 Sam 15). David's counsellor Ahithophel had gone over to the side of Absalom. "And it was told David, 'Ahithophel is among the conspirators with Absalom.' And David said, 'O LORD, please turn the counsel of Ahithophel into foolishness'" (2 Sam 15:31). David loved Absalom and did not want to kill him. This prayer was, then, a way of getting Absalom off the path of trying to be king without having him killed. The end result was not what David wanted, since Absalom was killed (2 Sam 18:14–15). However, David's prayer was answered in that Ahithophel's advice was not good. He told Absalom to sleep publicly with his father's concubines (2 Sam 16:20–22) and this resulted in the fulfilment of God's word of punishment for David's affair with Bathsheba (2 Sam 12:11–12).

It is not clear whether 2 Sam 21 falls in chronological order with the rest of the events within the book. But it nonetheless makes a point about prayer and seeking the LORD. The land was experiencing a long famine and David sought God regarding this. The LORD told him that the famine was the result of Saul's decision to kill the Gibeonites

(2 Sam 21:1). The Gibeonites wanted seven of Saul's descendants killed to avenge Saul putting the Gibeonites to death. David allowed this request, although he spared the son of Jonathan (2 Sam 21:2–9). After this, God answered prayer for the land again (2 Sam 21:14).

This incident seems utterly horrifying. No man should die for what his grandfather did. Indeed, the law of Moses actually forbids what David allowed the Gibeonites to do (Deut 24:16). In addition, David had made a promise to Saul regarding his descendants. Saul entreated David, "'Swear to me therefore by the LORD that you will not cut off my offspring after me, and that you will not destroy my name out of my father's house.' And David swore this to Saul" (1 Sam 24:21–22a).

The problem here was that, although the Gibeonites had a legitimate grievance against Saul that needed to be resolved, David did not pray about their request. Quite likely, things would have been wholly different had David prayed and asked the LORD instead of simply asking the Gibeonites what they wanted. The saga of the Gibeonites was a saga of lack of prayer all along. Joshua did not pray and hence the Gibeonites lived among Israel. Saul's killing of the Gibeonites is only recorded in this passage. We do know that Saul was rejected by God and God did not give him direction or wisdom. David should have known better and should have asked for wisdom. If the LORD could tell David what the problem was, he could have told David what the solution would be. If this is what happens when we do not consult God for a solution, then this should jolt us all into praying for wisdom. Don't approach major decisions without prayer, particularly ones that will seriously impact the lives of others. Don't proceed with decisions without considering what God has already said in his word. This is doubly applicable for Christian leaders.

Second Samuel 22 also appears out of place in the chronology of the book, because it refers to David singing a song when God delivered

him from Saul (2 Sam 22:1), when in fact Saul died before 2 Samuel
even begun. Nonetheless, the song teaches us something about prayer,
both positive and negative. David said, "I call upon the LORD, who is
worthy to be praised, and I am saved from my enemies" (2 Sam 22:4).
And again, "In my distress I called upon the LORD; to my God I
called. From his temple he heard my voice, and my cry came to his
ears" (2 Sam 22:7). David knew where to go for help when in trouble.
He went to the LORD, and he was delivered. In his time of fleeing
from the hand of Saul, David had choices to make on more than one
occasion. He could either dishonour God by killing Saul, the LORD's
anointed, or trust in God. He chose the latter (1 Sam 24; 26) and
therefore called upon God to help him. This is what the LORD did.

David's prayer to the LORD, and the LORD's favour in response,
contrasts with the fate of David's enemies. "They looked, but there was
none to save; they cried to the LORD, but he did not answer them"
(2 Sam 22:42). God was on David's side because he chose David as his
king. Those who opposed him found themselves acting in opposition to
God. This was the reason why they were not heard by God. Therefore,
if you want God to listen and answer, then do not be on the wrong side.
In the present, being on the right side is still a matter of being for God's
chosen king, but now that chosen king is the Lord Jesus Christ. Either
you are on the side of Jesus, or you are not heard by God.

The final incident during which David prayed was both the result of
his foolishness and an important step in the building of the temple (see
1 Chr 22:1; 2 Chr 3:1). The incident was itself somewhat paradoxical.
For reasons not stated in the text, the LORD was angry with Israel and
incited David to number the fighting men (2 Sam 24:1). This was a
foolish thing to do and Joab, the commander of David's army, knew this
(see Exod 30:12). Nonetheless, David was the king, and the fighting
men were numbered (2 Sam 24:2–4). Finally, David came to his senses
and prayed a prayer of repentance. "But David's heart struck him after

he had numbered the people. And David said to the LORD, 'I have sinned greatly in what I have done. But now, O LORD, please take away the iniquity of your servant, for I have done very foolishly'" (2 Sam 24:10). Unlike David's sin with Bathsheba, this did not require a prophet to bring his sin to his attention.

David was given three choices as punishment for this decision. David's response was that it was best to fall into the hands of the LORD. Therefore, the LORD sent a plague, killing seventy thousand people. As the angel was ready to destroy Jerusalem, the LORD stopped him. This was at the threshing floor of Araunah the Jebusite (2 Sam 24:11–16). "Then David spoke to the LORD when he saw the angel who was striking the people, and said, 'Behold, I have sinned, and I have done wickedly. But these sheep, what have they done? Please let your hand be against me and against my father's house'" (2 Sam 24:17). In this prayer, David recognised both his sin and his responsibility towards the people of Israel. His task as leader of Israel was to protect and guide them, not to put them in danger. This prayer of repentance is thus an example for Christian leaders when their actions have endangered those whom they have been tasked with shepherding. Let us pray in such a way as to take responsibility for our own choices and how these have affected others, particularly those who we have been given care over.

The prophet told David to build an altar on the threshing floor, which David then bought from Araunah. "And David built there an altar to the LORD and offered burnt offerings and peace offerings. So the LORD responded to the plea for the land, and the plague was averted from Israel" (2 Sam 24:25). The answer to David's prayer has several aspects to it. First of all, the site of the future temple appears to be the goal of this story. Secondly, the LORD had decided to stop the plague before David prayed. The fact that David was able to see the angel of destruction going towards Jerusalem implies that God gave him spiritual insight. His prayer was in response to this insight.

Thirdly, God told David to offer sacrifices. Burnt offerings were one form of sacrifice for sin (Lev 1). This makes sense given David's sin. However, peace (fellowship) offerings were not sacrifices for sin but voluntary offerings (see Lev 7:11–21), offered in this instance to thank God for his deliverance. These two types of offerings suggest that the LORD instigated the offerings so that the plague could stop because this was his intention. Not only does God's word precipitate prayer, but God works so that prayer can be answered. A sacrifice for sin is vital if anyone is to have fellowship with God through prayer, and we know that this sacrifice has been given to us in the cross. But God desires more than forgiveness; he wants us to know him, so the sacrifice of Christ opens the door to fellowship with God (compare 1 John 1:3).

A prayer of David is recorded in 1 Chr 29:10–19. Before his death, David provided as much as he could for the temple that Solomon would build later. After he had done all this, he prayed in front of all the people. David's prayer began with praise for who God is and what he is like. God is powerful and everything in heaven and earth belong to him. Therefore, he is exalted above all. He provides both wealth and honour because he is the ruler. Thanks are due to him. Then David went on to acknowledge that all the beautiful things that he and the people had provided to build the temple came from God in the first place. He offered these things back to God with uprightness of heart. There was then a plea for the God of Abraham, Isaac and Jacob to keep the hearts of God's people set on him, and that Solomon would have a heart to serve God and build the temple.

Although David had done a great deal of work to prepare for the temple, his prayer was focused on God's grace and provision and a hope that the people would continue to honour God. Like David, even when we work hard, it is good and right to exalt God, rather than ourselves, because we know that God has given us the very capacities which we offer back to him.

Conclusion

David's prayer life grew as David's life changed. As a warrior, he regularly consulted the LORD about battles he engaged in. But as he became settled as king, he began to pray differently. David's prayers became great psalms of praise to the God who had given him great promises. There were prayers of repentance also, although sometimes David needed prompting for these. He was bold enough to plead with God and humble enough to acknowledge God's greatness and power at work in his life. But even in the midst of this improved prayer life, there was a time when David failed to pray, with horrible consequences.

Like David, the situations in our lives change and we are able to grow our prayer lives. The secret to this growth, as in the life of David, is grasping God's promises and his character and work in our lives. As we understand this more and more, then greater prayers of praise will come from our lips. Let repentance be unbidden and may there be no times of failure to pray.

Reflection Questions / Journal Prompts

1. Do you regularly inquire of God for direction in your life? Consider what rhythms of prayer you can develop to make this a more consistent habit.
2. Meditate on the intense privilege of Christian prayer. Give thanks to the Father and the Lord Jesus Christ through the Holy Spirit for this privilege.
3. Make a list of what God has done for you, including salvation and non-salvation matters. Use this list to write a prayer of

praise to God.

4. Where do you go in times of trouble? If you do not first go to
God in prayer, consider why this is so.

The Prayer Life of Solomon

The prayer life of Solomon was marked by great highs and by dreadful lows. God was with Solomon to begin with. He was a great king like his father, David. He prayed great prayers like his father, David. But the greatness of his prayers did not rule out his slide into idolatry. This is an object lesson for us all.

Solomon Loved God

The slide into idolatry may have begun even as Solomon had established his reign and was building his palace. Solomon allied himself with the king of Egypt by marrying one of his daughters and brought her to Jerusalem (1 Kgs 3:1). Solomon would have known the law which forbids marrying a daughter of the nations around Israel because they will lead Israel into idolatry (Deut 7:2–4). Technically, Egyptian wives were not forbidden by this law. Were the gods of Egypt the beginning of Solomon's decline into idolatry? We don't know. However, at the point at which he married Pharaoh's daughter, Solomon loved the LORD God (1 Kgs 3:3).

Evidence of Solomon's love for God was found in the way Solomon prayed when God offered him a choice. When Solomon was in Gibeon offering sacrifices on the high place there, God appeared to him in a dream saying, "Ask me for whatever you want" (1 Kgs 3:4–5).

And Solomon said, "You have shown great and steadfast love to your servant David my father, because he walked before you in faithfulness, in righteousness, and in uprightness of heart toward you. And you have kept for him this great and steadfast love and have given him a son to sit on his throne this day. And now, O LORD my God, you have made your servant king in place of David my father, although I am but a little child. I do not know how to go out or come in. And your servant is in the midst of your people whom you have chosen, a great people, too many to be numbered or counted for multitude. Give your servant therefore an understanding mind to govern your people, that I may discern between good and evil, for who is able to govern this your great people?" (1 Kgs 3:6–9)

Solomon's prayer followed the pattern of the prayers of the patriarchs. He prayed because God first appeared to him in a dream. Instead of asking for something, Solomon recounted the love of God shown to him so far, first to David and then to Solomon as the one who sat on David's throne. Praise for the fulfilment of God's promises was an excellent beginning. Having thanked God for the throne, Solomon was humble enough to know his own weakness and therefore he asked for wisdom to govern. Even this request was couched in praise because the people he would govern were God's people, great in number because God had made them so according to his word. God was pleased with Solomon's prayer. He not only granted Solomon's request but also promised to give him wealth and honour. The final promise of long life had a caveat, that Solomon keep God's commands (1 Kgs 3:10–14). That God granted Solomon's request for wisdom to govern is demonstrated plainly in the story which follows of Solomon knowing how to discern which woman the baby belonged to (1 Kgs 3:16–28). His wisdom was beyond anyone else's (1 Kgs 4:29–34).

Most of us will not be kings of Israel or even be great leaders in the church or industry. But we can follow this pattern of prayer. Just as Solomon prayed in response to the word of God to him, we too must pray in response to God's word. In our case that word is found in the Bible. Praise is the right beginning to prayer. God's previous works in our lives and his faithfulness to his promises are a good basis for praise and a good foundation for requests. We do not need to be great leaders to realise our own weaknesses and pray for God to give us wisdom in the place he has put us. God will grant wisdom according to his promise (Jas 1:5). Many times, God also grants us what we had not dared to ask for.

Solomon Dedicated the Temple

Solomon's prayer at the dedication of the temple was lengthy, prophetic and wonderful. Building the temple was a long process (1 Kgs 6:37–38; 7:13–51). Finally, the ark was brought to the temple and Solomon recounted the events leading to the temple being built—from the word of God to the heart of David to the promise of David's son on the throne—and Solomon's provision of a place for the ark (1 Kgs 8:14–21). All of this was directed at the assembly of the people. But then Solomon prayed to the God of Israel (1 Kgs 8:22–53).

There were several elements to Solomon's temple dedication prayer. The first was acknowledgement that the God of Israel is uniquely God and that his promises to David had been fulfilled in the very building that was being dedicated. Then, Solomon asked that God's other promises to David, about his posterity and dynasty, would be similarly fulfilled by God (1 Kgs 8:23–26). We find this pattern of prayer repeated throughout the great prayers of the Old Testament saints—praising God for what he has done to fulfil his word and then asking that he would bring about other promises that had not yet been fulfilled.

The remaining parts of the prayer had as a focus a plea that when people pray in that temple, God would hear from heaven. This was summed up early in the prayer in this way.

"But will God indeed dwell on the earth? Behold, heaven and the highest heaven cannot contain you; how much less this house that I have built! Yet have regard to the prayer of your servant and to his plea, O LORD my God, listening to the cry and to the prayer that your servant prays before you this day, that your eyes may be open night and day toward this house, the place of which you have said, 'My name shall be there,' that you may listen to the prayer that your servant offers toward this place. And listen to the plea of your servant and of your people Israel, when they pray toward this place. And listen in heaven your dwelling place, and when you hear, forgive." (1 Kgs 8:27–30)

It was an incredible act of gracious condescension that God's name would come to dwell in the physical temple on earth. He fills more than heaven and earth. So, Solomon acknowledged to the LORD the greatness of God and the finiteness of the grand temple he spent seven years building. He knew full well that the God of Israel is not that small. It is fitting to remind ourselves as we pray that God is not small. A small god is a god who can be manipulated or moulded into our own likeness. The God who is too great to fit within the heavens themselves is the God worthy of worship and the God who is able to answer prayer for his people.

Even though the God of Israel cannot be contained in the temple or in the highest heaven, Solomon was bold enough to ask that God would hear and answer prayer offered towards that same temple. This plea was based on the promise, "My name shall be there". Solomon asked that day and night the LORD would pay attention to the temple and to the prayers prayed towards that place. God remains in heaven, but he hears from heaven. The rest of the prayer of Solomon considered the different scenarios that might result from there being a temple or praying towards the temple.

Solomon asked that God would judge between those who came to sort out disputes. He pleaded that God would listen when Israel had been defeated by an enemy due to their sin and yet turned to God in repentance. May the LORD hear, forgive and instruct those who repented when God sent no rain. He prayed for God to hear and forgive when any of God's people turned to him because of some plague or disaster. He asked that the LORD would listen to foreigners who came to the temple because they had heard of the glories of God's great name. May the LORD give success to Israel's armies when they prayed towards the temple. Finally, Solomon's prayer anticipated the day when Israel would sin so grievously against God that they would go into exile. Yet he asked that God would forgive and have mercy on those who repented in exile and turned back to the LORD from captivity (1 Kgs 8:31–51).

Solomon prayed, "'Let your eyes be open to the plea of your servant and to the plea of your people Israel, giving ear to them whenever they call to you. For you separated them from among all the peoples of the earth to be your heritage, as you declared through Moses your servant, when you brought our fathers out of Egypt, O Lord GOD'" (1 Kgs 8:52–53). The prayer ended with a plea for the LORD to listen no matter where his people called from because they were his people. Solomon appealed here to the fact of Israel's election, that is, God chose them and rescued them from Egypt.

Finally, let us consider Solomon's posture during this long prayer. "Then Solomon stood before the altar of the LORD in the presence of all the assembly of Israel and spread out his hands toward heaven" (1 Kgs 8:22). "Now as Solomon finished offering all this prayer and plea to the LORD, he arose from before the altar of the LORD, where he had knelt with hands outstretched toward heaven" (1 Kgs 8:54). He prayed before the altar of the LORD, the place of atonement (see, for example, Lev 4:26, 31, 35). The symbolism of this location is that one cannot approach God in prayer without atonement. The sacrifices that were offered on this day (1 Kgs 8:5) attest to this.

Secondly, Solomon spread out his hands towards heaven. This posture acknowledged that his prayer was directed towards the God who dwells in heaven, in unapproachable light (1 Tim 6:16). Solomon's final posture was kneeling, which suggests humility before the great God of heaven. All these physical gestures show that what we do with our bodies during prayer is indicative of what we think of God. This does not mean that there is only one place to pray or one posture to adopt. Kneeling has been a traditional posture of prayer, indicating our inferior position before God. It is, however, possible to pray standing, walking or sitting (e.g., Gen 18:22–23; 1 Chr 17:16).

Following the dedication of the temple, the LORD appeared to Solomon again, in the same way he had appeared at Gibeon (1 Kgs 9:1–2; see 1 Kgs 3:5). In this dream, "And the LORD said to him, 'I have heard your prayer and your plea, which you have made before me. I have consecrated this house that you have built, by putting my name there forever. My eyes and my heart will be there for all time'" (1 Kgs 9:3). The fact that the LORD affirmed he had heard the prayer of Solomon is quite wonderful. It means that the temple was not a mere human idea but one of which God approved. However, this affirmation of Solomon's prayer did not give Solomon license to do as he pleased as king. The LORD called him to have integrity of heart and to be obedient to God's law. God also warned that the temple would become a byword and the people cast into exile if they failed to obey God (1 Kgs 9:4–9). One godly prayer, answered by God, or even several such prayers, do not guarantee an ongoing walk with God. Diligence is needed.

Solomon Declined into Idol Worship

Diligence was precisely what Solomon failed in. Solomon did wondrous things in Israel and showed off his wealth—which was enormous—to the queen of Sheba (1 Kgs 9:10–10:29). However, he had a fatal flaw.

> Now King Solomon loved many foreign women, along with the daughter of Pharaoh: Moabite, Ammonite, Edomite, Sidonian, and Hittite women, from the nations concerning which the LORD had said to the people of Israel, "You shall not enter into marriage with them, neither shall they with you, for surely they will turn away your heart after their gods." Solomon clung to these in love. He had 700 wives, who were princesses, and 300 concubines. And his wives turned away his heart. (1 Kgs 11:1–3)

Solomon worshipped Ashtoreth, Chemosh and Molech, all because of his foreign wives. God was angry and promised to remove the kingdom from him (1 Kgs 11:4–11). The point of all this is that just because you have prayed and worshipped God faithfully for a time does not mean that the situation will necessarily remain as it is. If you allow yourself to be influenced by the wrong people, in contradiction to God's commands (compare 2 Cor 6:17), idolatry is easy to fall into. Then you may find yourself praying to gods which are nothing. Alternatively, the living God will have to discipline you to turn you back to true worship and prayer.

Conclusion

Solomon's kingship began with wholehearted devotion to God. Solomon prayed great and profound prayers, exalting the LORD and calling upon his mercy and faithfulness. But Solomon's reign ended with Solomon caught up in idol worship because of his poor choices of wives. We must beware. No matter how well we begin, it is always possible to end badly if we do not remain awake to the influences around us and the choices we make. Jesus exhorts us to this very thing because he is coming soon and unexpectedly (Rev 16:15).

Reflection Questions / Journal Prompts

1. Praise God for the opportunities he has given you, acknowledge your weaknesses, and ask God for help in doing what he has called you to.
2. Solomon listed a series of situations in which the people of God might find themselves in need of God's help. What are some situations in which you need God's help. Come to God with confidence because of Christ and ask for his help.
3. What does your posture in prayer say about what you think of God?
4. Are there people in your life who are dragging you away from the living God? What steps do you need to take to renew your devotion to God?

Prophets and the False Religion at Bethel and Dan

Because of Solomon's fall into idolatry, the kingdom was split into two: northern Israel and southern Judah. This occurred immediately after the death of Solomon. The northern tribes rebelled against Rehoboam son of Solomon, and set up their own king, Jeroboam. Jeroboam reasoned that if the people of the northern kingdom of Israel had to go to the temple in Jerusalem to sacrifice, they would become loyal to the king in Judah, Rehoboam. To prevent this happening, Jeroboam set up two golden calves, calling them the gods of Israel, and put one in Bethel and one in Dan. To complete this false religion, he set up festivals, appointed priests and offered sacrifices (1 Kgs 12:1–33). This false religious system in Israel was the focus of attention of many northern prophets of the LORD.

Prophets, along with kings and priests, had a mediatorial role within Israel in the Old Testament. This was why prophets were often asked to pray on behalf of others. The books of Kings have a significant concentration of prophets, compared to many other books of narrative history in the Old Testament. These prophets frequently denounced the false religion and idol worship of kings in Israel. The most famous of these prophets were Elijah and Elisha, both of whom ministered in the northern kingdom of Israel. The prayer lives of these prophets is the focus of this chapter.

An Unnamed Prophet

Not long after the inauguration of the false religious system, a man of God went to the altar in Bethel and prophesied against it. King Jeroboam tried to stop the man of God, but his hand shrivelled up (1

Kgs 13:1–5). "And the king said to the man of God, 'Entreat now the favour of the LORD your God, and pray for me, that my hand may be restored to me.' And the man of God entreated the LORD, and the king's hand was restored to him and became as it was before" (1 Kgs 13:6). Along with the fact that God's word came through the man of God, the prophet was able to pray and see the king healed. The king did not repent or change his heart regarding his false religion, but the prayer of the prophet still prevailed with the LORD. This is not unlike the situation with Moses and Pharaoh.

If we consider what Jesus said about the cities who would have repented at his miracles, incidents such as the healing of Jeroboam's hand, in which prayer was answered immediately, serve as an indication of further condemnation for those who see miracles and do not repent (Matt 11:21–24; Luke 10:13–16). Like Pharaoh, Jeroboam did not repent but wanted the prophet to pray to the LORD. They both continued in their wickedness as if God would just bail them out when necessary; there was no reverence or worship. Neither of these men prayed for themselves but asked the prophet to do it. We cannot take these amazingly quick answers to prayer as an indication of God being on their side. He was not. Both the affliction and the healing in answer to prayer show who is truly God and who was the prophet. It should drive someone to seek out the true God, but it did not in these cases.

Elijah

Elijah was possibly the greatest prophet in the Old Testament after Moses. He was a powerful prophet, feared by the kings with whom he had to do, beginning with Ahab. Yet Elijah also ministered to ordinary people. Having warned the king of Israel of an oncoming drought, and hidden for a time, Elijah went to Gentile territory. There he met a widow, who was miraculously fed and who fed Elijah (1 Kgs 17:1–16).

Later on, the woman's son died and in her grief she accused Elijah of reminding her of her sin and killing her son (1 Kgs 17:17–18).

> And he said to her, "Give me your son." And he took him from her arms and carried him up into the upper chamber where he lodged, and laid him on his own bed. And he cried to the LORD, "O LORD my God, have you brought calamity even upon the widow with whom I sojourn, by killing her son?" Then he stretched himself upon the child three times and cried to the LORD, "O LORD my God, let this child's life come into him again." And the LORD listened to the voice of Elijah. And the life of the child came into him again, and he revived. (1 Kgs 17:19–22)

The woman was a Gentile and thus had no real rights before the God of Israel, even though she had faith in God (1 Kgs 17:10–16). So she asked the prophet for help. Even the people of Israel would have asked the prophet for help, as we have seen in previous examples. But because of Christ, the position of Gentiles is now the same as the position of Jews before God (Eph 2:11–22). Indeed, through Christ, the Christian's access to God is far greater than that of an ancient Israelite, not to mention an ancient Gentile.

The answer to prayer in Elijah's case was quite unique in that he basically raised the dead. This was not a common event, either in the Old Testament or the New. Jesus raised three people from the dead (Jairus' daughter—Luke 8:40–56; the son of the widow of Nairn—Luke 7:11–17; and Lazarus—John 11), although he healed thousands. The apostle Peter raised Tabitha (Acts 9:36–43) from the dead and the apostle Paul raised Eutychus (Acts 20:7–12). We should not imagine that a request like this will often be answered in this way. Expecting a resurrection from the dead will likely leave us disappointed if not jaded. We can, however, have assurance in the general resurrection of the dead, when the Lord Jesus returns in glory and raises all believers to life eternal (Rom 8:11, 23).

Elijah's most famous action was on Mt Carmel. There he challenged the prophets of Baal to see whose god answered with fire. The prophets of Baal called upon their god for hours with no result. This went on until the time of the evening sacrifice (1 Kgs 18:16–29). Then it was Elijah's turn to call upon the LORD God of Israel. He repaired the altar, prepared the sacrifice and prayed.

> And at the time of the offering of the oblation, Elijah the prophet came near and said, "O LORD, God of Abraham, Isaac, and Israel, let it be known this day that you are God in Israel, and that I am your servant, and that I have done all these things at your word. Answer me, O LORD, answer me, that this people may know that you, O LORD, are God, and that you have turned their hearts back." Then the fire of the LORD fell and consumed the burnt offering and the wood and the stones and the dust, and licked up the water that was in the trench. (1 Kgs 18:36–38)

Elijah's prayer was at a particular time of day, the time of the evening sacrifice. Every day priests offered a morning and evening sacrifice (Exod 29:38–39) in addition to any sin offerings, guilt offerings, burnt offerings or fellowship offerings that people brought. This was a regular expression of worship in the tabernacle or temple. At the time that Elijah prophesied, there was a false sacrificial system in Israel, and even that was being ignored in favour of worshipping the false god Baal. Thus, God answered Elijah's prayer, prayed at the time of the evening sacrifice, because he wanted to demonstrate that his sacrificial system was the true way of worship, and he is the only true God.

Elijah asked that the LORD make himself known as God. The goal was the repentance of the people, their turning back to the true God of Israel. This was very much a kingdom prayer. Elijah did not ask for a miracle in order to bring glory to himself, but glory to the living God. He did not ask for a random miracle either. The particular miracle was totally in line with what God did in the tabernacle to show he had accepted the offering on the altar (see Lev 9:24; 2 Chr 7:1). Just as had happened in the tabernacle and the temple, the people fell on their faces and acknowledged that the LORD is the true God.

This sort of spectacular answer to prayer often engenders a degree of longing in our hearts to see something like this happen in our lives or in our country to convince people of the truth. This particular miracle was clearly not common in the Bible. As much as we may long for miracles every day, these were rare in the Bible and are rare in the present. Instead of seeing this miracle as the norm and having an expectation that all prayer must be answered in such spectacular fashion, it will be helpful to see how this miracle was fulfilled in the life of Christ.

Jesus died at the time of the evening sacrifice (Matt 27:45–50). He is the true God as well as the perfect sacrifice. Jesus is the lamb of God (John 1:29, 36), who offered himself on the altar (Heb 7:27; 9:14) as a pleasing aroma to God. The fire of God fell upon the sacrifice of Christ, but the fire Jesus spoke of (Luke 12:49) was for him a fire of God's holy wrath upon sin. The indication that his sacrifice was acceptable was not the cross itself, which looked like God's curse (Gal 3:13). Instead, it was the resurrection of Jesus from the grave on the third day (Rom 1:4). Since his death and resurrection are the basis of all answered prayer, this fulfillment should change the way we see the miracle that Elijah received. Christian believers have become an acceptable sacrifice on the altar because we are in Christ (Rom 12:1; 1 Pet 2:5). The tongues of fire on the church on the Day of Pentecost (Acts 2:3) were the fire of God which demonstrated that the church is an acceptable sacrifice to God.

Sadly, Elijah's final prayers were not particularly full of faith. After the grand demonstration of God's power on Mt Carmel, Elijah ran away from Queen Jezebel, who had threatened to kill him. Elijah went into the wilderness and sat under a bush (1 Kgs 19:1–4). He was clearly depressed. "And he asked that he might die, saying, 'It is enough; now, O LORD, take away my life, for I am no better than my fathers'" (1 Kgs 19:4b). An angel ministered to Elijah and sent him to Horeb (1 Kgs 19:5–8). There the LORD initiated a conversation with Elijah. "There he came to a cave and lodged in it. And behold, the word of the LORD came to him, and he said to him, 'What are you doing here, Elijah?' He said, 'I have been very jealous for the LORD, the God of hosts. For the people of Israel have forsaken your covenant, thrown down your altars, and killed your prophets with the sword, and I, even I only, am left, and they seek my life, to take it away'" (1 Kgs 19:9–10). This same question and answer are repeated in verses 13–14.

Elijah wanted to die and asked the LORD for this. As much as Elijah wanted to die, he did not want Jezebel to kill him, which is the irony of this whole narrative. Nonetheless, Elijah's prayers here were answered in several different ways. First of all, the LORD took Elijah's prayer to die seriously. He gave Elijah instructions for anointing of kings, which was one of the tasks assigned to prophets. This was in a way an instruction to keep living for now. But God also told Elijah to anoint Elisha as his successor, implying that his death was not too long away. Thirdly, the LORD encouraged Elijah by pointing out that God is sovereign over all. "Yet I will leave seven thousand in Israel, all the knees that have not bowed to Baal, and every mouth that has not kissed him" (1 Kgs 19:18). Elijah thought that the situation in Israel was hopeless, with so many apostates, but nonetheless God's purposes would be accomplished.

Elijah's Successor, Elisha

Elijah was succeeded by Elisha. Elisha's first recorded prayer was prayed just before Elijah died. Elijah had been told earlier to anoint Elisha as his successor. When Elijah went to Elisha, Elisha burned his ploughing equipment and the cattle attached to it and followed Elijah as his servant (1 Kgs 19:16, 19–21). Hence Elisha was God's chosen prophet. At the time approaching Elijah's death, there was no indication of how powerful Elisha would become as a prophet. But Elisha knew that he wanted to be a prophet like Elijah, and even greater than him. When Elijah asked Elisha what he could do for him before he was taken away, Elisha asked for a double portion of Elijah's spirit (2 Kgs 2:9). If this was a reference to the Holy Spirit, who anoints and empowers prophets, then Elijah could not have made this happen. Therefore, Elisha's request might be considered a prayer uttered to and through the prophet. At that point, Elisha did not yet have the authority of a prophet.

But after Elijah had been taken to heaven in a whirlwind, Elisha could then utter his prayer directly to the LORD with confidence. Like Moses (who parted the Red Sea—Exod 14) and Joshua (who parted the Jordan—Josh 3) before him, Elisha struck the Jordan River with Elijah's cloak and prayed, "Where is the LORD, the God of Elijah?" and the water parted (2 Kgs 2:11–14). "Where is the LORD, the God of Elijah?" is a prayer that God would be with him in the same way he was with Elijah. It is somewhat indirect. But it was answered in a powerful way. Now that Elijah was dead, Elisha was the one through whom God spoke. People would begin to inquire of God through him. It was the beginning of his prophetic authority. From this point onward, Elisha was the powerful prophet.

In the vein of Elijah, Elisha did many miracles. These were generally done without any signs of prayer. We are given only occasional glimpses of Elisha's prayer life. One particular instance involved praying for a dead child. Elisha was ministered to by a woman in Shunem. She fed him and provided a small room for him to stay in as he travelled that way. Elisha asked her if he could help her in return; could he put in a good word with the king or the commander of the army? What she wanted was a son. Elisha promised that she would have one within a year (2 Kgs 4:8–17). Did the prophet have the power to make such a thing happen? He spoke the word of prophecy with all the authority of God's word, implying that it was God's word. Perhaps instead of asking the king for a favour, he asked the LORD for a favour for this woman. In other words, he prayed.

The same child later died. The Shunammite went to Elisha. He knew something was wrong, but God did not reveal it to him. When she told him that there was a problem with her son, he sent Gehazi, his servant, to lay his staff on the boy's face. Gehazi did what he was told but the boy did not get up. Gehazi did not have the authority of the prophet and even the staff of the prophet was not sufficient to provide the miracle (2 Kgs 4:18–31). "When Elisha came into the house, he saw the child lying dead on his bed. So he went in and shut the door behind the two of them and prayed to the LORD" (2 Kgs 4:32–33). There was no doubt that Elisha had no power to raise the dead without prayer. He knew that he needed the LORD to do the miracle, and hence he prayed.

Another event in Elisha's ministry specifically involved no prayer. When Naaman the Syrian came to the prophet Elisha to be cured of his serious skin disease, Elisha did not even come out to meet him, but sent a messenger to tell him to dip himself in the Jordan seven times (2 Kgs 5:1–10). "But Naaman was angry and went away, saying, 'Behold, I thought that he would surely come out to me and stand and call upon the name of the LORD his God, and wave his hand over the place and cure the leper'" (2 Kgs 5:11). It perhaps seems strange that Elisha did not pray for Naaman at all. But what happened here is not necessarily what it seems. Elisha was a man of God and he likely prayed quite regularly. In this case, he did not do so publicly. Possibly this was because Naaman was expecting a certain religious ritual like what he saw back in his home country. His god, Rimmon, was possibly like Baal, and we know that there were loud rituals associated with Baal worship (see 1 Kgs 18:26). Perhaps Elisha did not pray in public precisely because he intended to separate himself from the expectations of Naaman.

Jesus cautioned us against loud and gaudy public rituals of prayer, but instead commanded, "But when you pray, go into your room and shut the door and pray to your Father who is in secret. And your Father who sees in secret will reward you" (Matt 6:6). There are times for prayer in public and times when it is best not to give in to the desires of people for pomp and ritual, neither of which need be part of genuine prayer to the true God. He is not impressed by such things.

Yet on another occasion, Elisha prayed in the hearing of his servant. The king of Aram (Syria) regularly staged incursions into Israel, but each time Elisha knew where he was camped, and warned the king of Israel. The king of Aram thought he had a traitor in his midst, but his officers claimed it was Elisha the prophet who was to blame. Hence the king sent some men to capture Elisha. When they arrived, they surrounded the city and Elisha's servant was afraid. However, Elisha was not afraid because he could see the angelic armies protecting them. "Then Elisha prayed and said, 'O LORD, please open his eyes that he may see.' So the LORD opened the eyes of the young man, and he saw, and behold, the mountain was full of horses and chariots of fire all around Elisha" (2 Kgs 6:17).

Because of his calling as a prophet, Elisha could see what others could not. He knew that his servant would be unable to see the angelic armies unless his eyes were opened by the LORD himself. Such stories ignite in some people a desire to see supernatural beings. It should be noted here that seeing supernatural beings was not an end in itself. The purpose was that the servant would understand what Elisha understood and also to see what God was doing. The following story in this very chapter (the siege of Samaria and severe famine, followed by deliverance) demonstrates that God's intervention in the life of Israel was not always so obviously supernatural. It would do us no good, then, to focus our prayers continually on the desire to see angels. Better that we focus on spiritual insight into what God is doing in the church, whether that be something obviously miraculous or something less obvious but no less powerful, like sanctification. That said, there may be times when it is appropriate to pray a prayer similar to this prayer of Elisha. Learn to follow the lead of the Holy Spirit.

Several prayers followed this. Elisha's desire was for the LORD to demonstrate his sovereignty over the Syrian army. The Syrians were under the impression that their might and power made them invincible. But God sees where no one else sees and hears what is said behind closed doors.

> And when the Syrians came down against him, Elisha prayed to the LORD and said, "Please strike this people with blindness." So he struck them with blindness in accordance with the prayer of Elisha. And Elisha said to them, "This is not the way, and this is not the city. Follow me, and I will bring you to the man whom you seek." And he led them to Samaria. As soon as they entered Samaria, Elisha said, "O LORD, open the eyes of these men, that they may see." So the LORD opened their eyes and they saw, and behold, they were in the midst of Samaria. (2 Kgs 6:18–20)

The soldiers found themselves in front of the king of Samaria and very vulnerable. The king fed them and sent them home. This experience led to the end of the raids by Syria, at least for a time.

Conclusion

Elijah was a powerful prophet, whose prayers resulted in the dead being raised and fire coming down from heaven. Elisha was similarly a powerful prophet. They stand as types of Christ. In other words, they show us something of what the Messiah, Jesus, would be. In this sense, the miracles that Elijah and Elisha are not given as direct examples for Christians to follow. They simply point forward to the greatest prophet of all, the one through whom God speaks and who is the Word of God incarnate.

The powerful nature of their ministry might make the prayer life of either prophet seem out of bounds for ordinary people like you and me. But the New Testament affirms that Elijah was an ordinary human being (Jas 5:17). Consequently, Elijah and Elisha offer us an example of confidence in coming to God in prayer. As Christians we don't need a prophet to pray on our behalf. Through Christ we can come to God with boldness and confidence (Heb 4:16; 10:19–22). God is able to work powerfully through the prayers of his people when we come to him in faith. Therefore, let us be bold and ask God to move in his church, to display his glory and his sovereign power among his people.

Reflection Questions / Journal Prompts

1. Jeroboam did not repent when prayer was answered. What is your response to answered prayer: praise or contempt for God?
2. Give thanks to God that the church is an acceptable offering to God. Consider what it means to offer yourself to God as a

sacrifice. How does that change your thinking about how you live?

3. In what situations is public prayer best? In what situations is private prayer best and public prayer to be avoided?

4. Meditate on the truth that Elijah was a man like us. Describe how this truth can provide you with confidence to ask God for anything.

Some Kings with Substandard Prayer Lives

G od gave Israel kings to rule over them. These kings were always intended to rule under God and to lead the people to stay faithful to the true God. Unfortunately, many of the kings of Israel and Judah were wicked idol-worshippers and led the nation astray. The prayer lives of several kings stand out as really terrible. Hopefully, their terrible examples will help us to gain wisdom to do the opposite.

God's Sovereignty over a Lack of Prayer

When Solomon died, his son Rehoboam became king. When people came to him with a complaint, he consulted the elders, but he did not ask the LORD what to do. He rejected the advice of the elders and instead took the advice of his young advisors (1 Kgs 12:1–14). "So the king did not listen to the people, for it was a turn of affairs brought about by the LORD that he might fulfill his word, which the LORD spoke by Ahijah the Shilonite to Jeroboam the son of Nebat" (1 Kgs 12:15). Ahijah had told Jeroboam son of Nebat (an official of Solomon) that the LORD would make him king over ten out of twelve tribes of Israel (1 Kgs 11:26–39). The division of Israel into two kingdoms occurred because Rehoboam was foolish and did not listen to good advice, nor did he pray to the LORD.

Wicked kings did not ask the LORD for wisdom, as a general rule. The result here was both dreadful and according to the will of God. What theology of prayer can we take from this? God is sovereign. As we have seen, when the LORD desired to save his people, whether those in Israel or those associated with Israel, he did not allow circumstances to prevent his will from being accomplished. One of the themes we have seen in the prayers of some significant people so far is that God prompted them to pray when a situation needed it so that people would be delivered. But God is equally sovereign over the wicked as he is over his own people, those who have faith. This means that the failure of Rehoboam to pray for wisdom is just as much a part of God's sovereign plan to accomplish his will as the times when he incited godly people to pray. Since it was God's will to divide Israel into two kingdoms, he used Rehoboam's pride and prayerlessness to bring about this event.

Asa Slid into Prayerlessness

Asa king of Judah started out as a king with a good prayer life and ended as a king with an abysmal prayer life. Early in his reign, Asa was concerned to rid Judah of its idols, and he commanded the people of Judah to seek the LORD (2 Chr 14:2–5). When Zerah the Ethiopian sent an army against Judah, Asa and his army went out to meet him (2 Chr 14:9–10). "And Asa cried to the LORD his God, 'O LORD, there is none like you to help, between the mighty and the weak. Help us, O LORD our God, for we rely on you, and in your name we have come against this multitude. O LORD, you are our God; let not man prevail against you'" (2 Chr 14:11). Prayer to the LORD was Asa's response to the threat. He appealed to the uniqueness of God as the helper of the weak. The LORD helped Asa; the Ethiopians fled, and Judah plundered the Ethiopians (2 Chr 14:12–13).

After this, God sent a prophet to Asa with a promise and a warning. "Hear me, Asa, and all Judah and Benjamin: The LORD is with you while you are with him. If you seek him, he will be found by you, but if you forsake him, he will forsake you" (2 Chr 15:2b–c). Inspired and encouraged by these words Asa made reforms in Judah, Benjamin and the towns he had captured in Ephraim. He made a covenant with the people to seek the LORD and deposed his idolatrous grandmother (2 Chr 15:8–18). However, this zeal did not last his whole life.

Late in his life, Asa made a treaty with Ben-Hadad king of Aram, who then attacked Israel instead of Judah (2 Chr 16:1–6).

> At that time Hanani the seer came to Asa king of Judah and said to him, "Because you relied on the king of Syria, and did not rely on the LORD your God, the army of the king of Syria has escaped you. Were not the Ethiopians and the Libyans a huge army with very many chariots and horsemen? Yet because you relied on the LORD, he gave them into your hand. For the eyes of the LORD run to and fro throughout the whole earth, to give strong support to those whose heart is blameless toward him. You have done foolishly in this, for from now on you will have wars." (2 Chr 16:7–9)

The earlier trust in the LORD and prayer to him in times of need were no longer present in Asa. Because he acted instead of praying first, Asa would have to suffer the consequences, in this case constantly being at war. The state of Asa's heart in relation to the LORD was further revealed by the fact that he imprisoned the prophet who rebuked him (2 Chr 16:10).

The consequences of his failure to pray did not turn Asa back to the LORD. A few years later, he was afflicted with a disease of his feet. But he did not pray. "In the thirty-ninth year of his reign Asa was diseased in his feet, and his disease became severe. Yet even in his disease he did not seek the LORD, but sought help from physicians" (2 Chr 16:12). This was not a slight on medical practitioners of the kind we are used to. The physicians referred to here relied on incantations and idolatrous practices for healing. The problem was Asa's failure to seek the LORD in prayer.

The narrative of Asa's reign in 1 Kgs 15 does not mention Asa's fall away from love for God. Nonetheless, we are given insight in 2 Chronicles into the danger that exists for all of us. The prophet's warning to Asa—"If you seek him, he will be found by you, but if you forsake him, he will forsake you"—must be taken to heart. It is quite possible that a Christian can start out loving God and praying to him, seeking God in good and in trouble, as Asa did, and yet end without a prayer life. We do not know what turned Asa from a man with a good prayer life to a man without one. It is vital, then, to be diligent and pay attention to any slide into prayerlessness. One day without prayer can turn into two and three, then weeks become years. Trust in God must be practised not presumed upon. Just because our Christian lives began well does not mean that they will end that way.

Ahab: No Interest in Prayer

Late in Asa's reign, Ahab became king of Israel (1 Kgs 16:29). King Ahab was threatened by Ben-Hadad, who demanded all his silver and gold as well as his wives and children. When Ben-Hadad upped his demands, Ahab refused to comply. Then Ben-Hadad got ready to attack. At this point a prophet came to Ahab and told him that God would give him victory over the Arameans, which he did. But Ben-Hadad lived to fight again. The next spring, he came back with a stronger army. The Arameans thought that the God of Israel was a god of the hills, so they believed they could have success against Israel on the plains (1 Kgs 20:1–27). "And a man of God came near and said to the king of Israel, 'Thus says the LORD, "Because the Syrians have said, 'The LORD is a god of the hills but he is not a god of the valleys,' therefore I will give all this great multitude into your hand, and you shall know that I am the LORD"'" (1 Kgs 20:28). This is exactly what God did.

What looked like a spectacular answer to prayer was not that at all because there was no prayer at all. Ahab was a wicked king, more wicked than any king before him. He had a wicked wife and they both worshipped several false gods (1 Kgs 16:30–33). If he prayed at all, it is not recorded. Yet the LORD gave two amazing victories to Ahab's armies to demonstrate his own glory, rather than because of Ahab's trust in God, which was non-existent. Why does God do amazing things in the lives of people who are not godly, while godly people experience seemingly unanswered prayer? Perhaps it is for this reason, to demonstrate to the ungodly that there is a real God in heaven to whom they are accountable. The godly are often sanctified through having to persist in prayer when there is no answer.

Ahab's poor attitude towards seeking the LORD was demonstrated again when he allied himself with Jehoshaphat king of Judah. Before they went to war together, Jehoshaphat wanted to inquire of the LORD through a prophet. The kind of prophets Ahab asked for were all yes-men, who told him what he wanted to hear. Jehoshaphat insisted on a prophet of the LORD, and they found Micaiah. This kind of inquiry was not prayer in the Christian sense since no one spoke to God directly. However, a lot of Old Testament prayer was inquiring of God through a prophet or a priest, as we have already seen. The answer to the inquiry was not what anyone wanted to hear. Micaiah prophesied Ahab's death in battle. Ahab thought he could somehow outsmart the word from God through the prophet. He died in battle anyway (1 Kgs 22:1–40).

The lesson from this story about Ahab is that it is foolish to inquire of God if you do not want to hear the answer that he gives. Ahab never wanted to know what God said, which is why he was surrounded by false prophets. His attitude did not change after he heard what God said. If you are going to pray and ask God for direction, then don't ignore the direction he gives, whether that be through the Bible or through others.

Ahaziah's Prayer to a False God

The next king of Israel also failed to seek the LORD in prayer. "Now Ahaziah fell through the lattice in his upper chamber in Samaria, and lay sick; so he sent messengers, telling them, 'Go, inquire of Baal-zebub, the god of Ekron, whether I shall recover from this sickness'" (2 Kgs 1:2). The word "inquire" here is sometimes used of inquiring of the LORD (e.g., 1 Sam 9:9; 1 Kgs 22:7; 2 Kgs 3:11; 8:8). But Ahaziah was like his father, Ahab, in that he was wicked and served and worshipped Baal (1 Kgs 22:52–53). I don't know how the inquiry was made of the idol, but I assume the priests of Baal-zebub had a ritual of sorts to find out the answer. The important point was that this king prayed to the wrong god. As a consequence, Elijah was sent to ask him why he consulted a foreign idol when the true God was in Israel. Because of his idolatry, Ahaziah would not recover from his injury. The LORD does not countenance rivals or those who worship them.

There is a temptation, to which Ahaziah succumbed, to pray to a false god because that god does not have the same requirements as the true and living God. The holiness of the true God is formidable and scary. What if God requires something of me and I do not want to obey him? What if my sin must be repented of? A made-up god can have different expectations, ones which I get to choose. Although Christians do not want to admit to worshipping idols, it is not out of the ordinary to find ourselves wondering why the god we have made in our own heads does not answer our prayers. This is an opportunity for repentance and to turn back to the truth about God as given to us in the Bible. Ahaziah did not repent because he did not want to serve the God of Israel.

Three Different Understandings of Prayer

Sometime later, the king of Moab rebelled against the king of Israel. The responses of three different kings demonstrated three different understandings of prayer. Jehoram (aka Joram) king of Israel was the son of Ahab, but not quite as wicked as his father. When the king of Moab rebelled, Jehoram asked Jehoshaphat king of Judah to fight against Moab. The king of Edom also joined them. None of these kings is recorded as inquiring of the LORD before embarking upon this battle. After a week of marching, they ran out of water. The king of Israel lamented that God seemed to have called them together to die in the battle with Moab (2 Kgs 3:1–10). He did not pray. His upbringing was obviously not a godly one and Jehoram was not accustomed to asking the LORD for help, even though he was happy to utter his name. He simply acted on the basis of his own decision-making skills, not on the basis of God's leading.

But Jehoshaphat asked for a prophet so they could inquire of the LORD. Elisha was there but initially refused to inquire of the LORD for the king of Israel, instead telling him to ask the prophets of his father and mother (2 Kgs 3:11–13). "And Elisha said, 'As the LORD of hosts lives, before whom I stand, were it not that I have regard for Jehoshaphat the king of Judah, I would neither look at you nor see you'" (2 Kgs 3:14). Wicked kings had no right to inquire of the LORD and expect to be heard. This was not a direct prayer as such, but the same principle applies. You cannot give yourself over to the worship of false gods and then pray to the true God when it suits you. The LORD hears only those who are his, who worship and serve him alone.

Because Jehoshaphat was a good king, God gave them instructions, they were given water, and the battle against Moab was won (2 Kgs 3:14–25). Then we find out what the king of Moab thought was a sensible way to pray. The king of Moab saw that he was losing and tried one last time to overcome but failed (2 Kgs 3:26). "Then he took his oldest son who was to reign in his place and offered him for a burnt offering on the wall. And there came great wrath against Israel. And they withdrew from him and returned to their own land" (2 Kgs 3:27). The Moabite king thought that human sacrifice would turn the battle in his favour. This is not in keeping with God's character at all. God states plainly that human sacrifice never entered his mind (Jer 32:35). Several false gods in the Ancient Near East—Chemosh, Baal and Molech—had human sacrifice as part of their worship. But the true and living God did not ask for such a thing. (Note that although the LORD asked Abraham to sacrifice Isaac, he stopped him before the deed was done—Gen 22.) For this reason, we need to carefully consider our worship of and prayer to God, so that we do not assume he requires of us some horrendous deed in order to be heard.

Another Failure to Pray

Our next king with a poor prayer life is not named in the text, presumably because his part in the story was in the background. He had been the subject of a series of attempted incursions by the king of Aram. The prophet Elisha first thwarted these by warning the king where the enemy was camped. Then Elisha prayed for the enemy to become blind and led them to the king (2 Kgs 6:8–23). Having seen such miracles, it seems beyond belief that this particular king did not pray when the situation became dire. However, sometime after the above events, the king of Aram laid siege to the city of Samaria. As was customary in these ancient sieges, the city was cut off and food became incredibly scarce. So much so that a woman went to the king to complain that she had made a pact with another woman to eat their children. They had eaten her child, but the other woman had hidden her son. The king did not know what to do. Instead of praying to the LORD for help, as several other kings before and after him did, he cursed Elisha and threatened to kill him (2 Kgs 6:24–31). The

LORD showed his kindness to his people by bringing a miraculous deliverance, despite the apparent lack of prayer on the part of the king (2 Kgs 7).

When disaster of this magnitude strikes, prayer must be our first port of call. We may not have had such spectacular miracles to draw on as this unnamed king, but there are many miracles in the Bible to remind us of what God has done and can do. It has not been my experience that God immediately and miraculously removes all the difficulties in life. However, it seems utterly foolhardy to ignore the help we might receive from him by failing to turn to him in a crisis.

God's Mercy

Manasseh was a wicked king. He rebuilt altars to idols that his father had torn down. He sacrificed to false gods, practiced divination, offered his children to idols, put idols in the LORD's temple, and engaged in many other ungodly practices. The LORD spoke to Manasseh and his people but there was no repentance. So the LORD brought the Assyrians against Judah and they captured king Manasseh and took him to Babylon (2 Chr 33:1–11). "And when he was in distress, he entreated the favour of the LORD his God and humbled himself greatly before the God of his fathers. He prayed to him, and God was moved by his entreaty and heard his plea and brought him again to Jerusalem into his kingdom. Then Manasseh knew that the LORD was God" (2 Chr 33:12–13).

By all accounts Manasseh was an ungodly man and, before his deportation to Babylon, his prayers would have been to the false gods of surrounding nations. However, despite his wickedness, it was to the LORD that he prayed when he was in serious trouble. We see here how great God's mercy is. It served to demonstrate to Manasseh who is the true God. Even wicked people may have prayer answered if there is repentance. Sometimes it takes something deeply distressing for people to turn to the LORD and pray. Pride keeps people from praying. In fact, the dreadful judgement Manasseh experienced was necessary because prior to this he relied completely on idols. We may not be able to say that Manasseh repented such that he was saved in an eternal sense. But the passage implies that he worshipped the LORD and cast aside his idols. Negative experiences, then, whether the difficulty is small or great, are an opportunity given by God to provoke us to repentance and bring us back to reliance on him. Prayer is a significant part of that repentance.

Conclusion

When it comes to having a poor prayer life there are several options. A person might start out well and decline into prayerlessness. Another might experience the power of God to deliver for no other reason than God decided to demonstrate his own glory. One might seek after false gods. Another might be wicked and presume upon God to answer his prayer, even though God does not bless wickedness. Some think prayer requires all manner of extreme means to twist God's arm. Lastly, a poor prayer life might mean nothing more complex than a simple failure to ask for God's help, even in a crisis. We must guard against these poor examples. Although God is far more gracious than we can imagine, a lack of prayer usually means a lack of help from the only one who can truly be called the helper of Israel (Hos 13:9; compare Ps 30:10).

Reflection Questions / Journal Prompts

1. Think about times when God's sovereign hand was very evident in your circumstances. Thank God in faith for the times when his sovereignty was less evident.
2. Consider whether there are symptoms of a slide into prayerlessness in your life. Do you pray less than you did at first? Do you avoid praying even when in trouble? Repent if

necessary.

3. Recall a time when you asked God for guidance but had already made up your mind what you would do. What was the result?

4. It is never too late to turn to God in prayer. Are there situations which you have avoided bringing to the Father in heaven? Hesitate no more.

Kings with Better Prayer Lives

Rarely in Kings and Chronicles do we find a king who does what pleases the LORD and who seeks God instead of using only political schemes to survive. Even among kings, prayer seems to be a rarity. However, there are a few kings who have God-honouring prayer lives. These put their trust in the living God. They expressed devotion to God and encouraged others to do the same. These are some we may emulate.

Hezekiah's Kingdom Prayer and Prayer for Healing

Hezekiah was a good king, who did what was right in the eyes of the LORD. He removed the high places and smashed idols. He was obedient to God, and God was with him. He was successful in battle and courageous enough to rebel against the Assyrians. In the fourth year of his reign the king of Assyria attacked Samaria, captured it after three years, and took Israel into exile. This happened due to their sin and violation of the LORD's covenant. But then a serious problem arose for Hezekiah, namely, the king of Assyria attacked and captured the fortified cities of Judah (2 Kgs 18:1–13). The question in the mind of the reader is: Will Judah be going into exile as Israel did not long before?

Although Hezekiah was a God-honouring king like David, at first, he did not pray about the Assyrian problem but rather tried to appease the king of Assyria with an extremely large amount of silver and gold, stripped from the temple and the palace. Thus, he became a vassal of the Assyrians again (2 Kgs 18:14–16). It would take an even larger threat for Hezekiah to be desperate enough to seek the LORD's help.

Given what God would eventually do in response to prayer, we have to wonder why Hezekiah did not get to prayer faster. However, we might ask the same thing about ourselves when faced with some difficulty. How long does it take before we stop relying on human methods to solve the problem and turn to God in prayer?

But the king of Assyria, Sennacherib, was not satisfied with only part of Judah under his belt and came to take Jerusalem. He sent military officials and an army to Jerusalem, and they spoke to Hezekiah's ministers. The word from the field commander was a taunt to those in Jerusalem. He stated plainly that they could not rely on Egypt to help them, nor could they rely on the LORD their God. The boast was that even if the Assyrians gave the army of Jerusalem extra horses and riders, the Assyrians would still destroy them. They then made false promises about what would happen if the people of Jerusalem surrendered, and they reiterated that neither king Hezekiah nor the LORD himself could be trusted to deliver Jerusalem from the hands of the mighty Assyrian army. None of the gods of other nations were able to keep the Assyrians at bay (2 Kgs 18:17–35).

It was not until Hezekiah heard the reports of his ministers that he did anything at all. Finally, he tore his clothes (a sign of grief) and went to the temple. He sent his ministers to the prophet Isaiah with the hope of some help from the LORD. His message to Isaiah was that this was a time of great distress (2 Kgs 19:1–3). He said, "It may be that the LORD your God heard all the words of the Rabshakeh [field commander—NIV], whom his master the king of Assyria has sent to mock the living God, and will rebuke the words that the LORD your God has heard; therefore lift up your prayer for the remnant that is left" (2 Kgs 19:4). At first, Hezekiah did not pray himself but asked the prophet to do so. Since prophets had a mediatorial role this was not an unusual thing to do. Hezekiah hoped that the LORD would intervene because the Assyrians had ridiculed the LORD.

The word of God came through Isaiah that there would be deliverance. Then there was a temporary reprieve as the king of Assyria went to fight against Libnah (2 Kgs 19:5–8). But the Assyrians sent yet another message to Hezekiah.

> "Thus shall you speak to Hezekiah king of Judah: 'Do not let your God in whom you trust deceive you by promising that Jerusalem will not be given into the hand of the king of Assyria. Behold, you have heard what the kings of Assyria have done to all lands, devoting them to destruction. And shall you be delivered? Have the gods of the nations delivered them, the nations that my fathers destroyed, Gozan, Haran, Rezeph, and the people of Eden who were in Telassar? Where is the king of Hamath, the king of Arpad, the king of the city of Sepharvaim, the king of Hena, or the king of Ivvah?'" (2 Kgs 19:10–13)

This message repeated the same slanderous insult to the LORD that was delivered in 2 Kgs 18:33–34, but this time the message was directed at Hezekiah to discourage him from fighting back.

This dreadful message did not stop Hezekiah from asking for the LORD's help. Finally, he prayed himself. He took the message to the temple and spread it out before God (2 Kgs 19:14).

> And Hezekiah prayed before the LORD and said: "O LORD, the God of Israel, enthroned above the cherubim, you are the God, you alone, of all the kingdoms of the earth; you have made heaven and earth. Incline your ear, O LORD, and hear; open your eyes, O LORD, and see; and hear the words of Sennacherib, which he has sent to mock the living God. Truly, O LORD, the kings of Assyria have laid waste the nations and their lands and have cast their gods into the

fire, for they were not gods, but the work of men's hands, wood and stone. Therefore they were destroyed. So now, O LORD our God, save us, please, from his hand, that all the kingdoms of the earth may know that you, O LORD, are God alone." (2 Kgs 19:15–19)

The king was desperate for help from God, but his was not a prayer of despair but faith. His appeal was based on the truth that the God of Israel alone is God and there is no other. He is the God above all the earth because he is the Creator and worshipped by heavenly beings. Of course, all the gods of the nations around could not save from the Assyrians. They were not true gods but made of wood and stone. The LORD is the living God, and he can save. Hezekiah reminded God of what Sennacherib said about the LORD. It was not that God had forgotten but that the words of Sennacherib were an insult to God. Thus, Hezekiah was appealing to God's desire to show himself God among the nations of the earth. Consequently, Hezekiah's final plea was that God would save Jerusalem to demonstrate to all the kingdoms of the earth that he is God and there is no other. This prayer, like some others before it, is a kingdom prayer, a prayer whose foundation is the glory of God.

The prophet Isaiah sent word to Hezekiah that the LORD had heard his prayer. He prophesied against the Assyrians and delivered a promise that the LORD would defend the city of Jerusalem. The angel of the LORD killed thousands of Assyrian troops. Later the king of Assyria was assassinated by his own sons (2 Kgs 19:20–37).

Kingdom prayers, that focus on the glory of God instead of on our needs and desires, are prayers which God often answers powerfully in Scripture. We cannot know whether the situation would have been different if Hezekiah prayed the first time he was concerned about the king of Assyria or not. But we do know that the LORD is concerned to uphold his own glory in a godless world (Isa 42:8; 48:11; Ezek 39:21). Very few kings engaged in prayer like this. Even if Hezekiah did not at first call out to the LORD for help, his prayer is still a good example for us as to how to pray in a dire situation.

There is another prayer of Hezekiah recorded for our instruction. At this time, Hezekiah became seriously ill, and Isaiah confirmed that he would soon die (2 Kgs 20:1). "Then Hezekiah turned his face to the wall and prayed to the LORD, saying, 'Now, O LORD, please remember how I have walked before you in faithfulness and with a whole heart, and have done what is good in your sight.' And Hezekiah wept bitterly" (2 Kgs 20:2–3). Here Hezekiah asked God to extend his life based on his own personal piety. God was gracious and healed Hezekiah through the prophet, and Hezekiah lived another fifteen years (2 Kgs 20:4–7).

There are a few questions regarding this prayer. This type of prayer only makes sense because Hezekiah was a good king who really desired to honour the LORD. It would not have been a helpful way to pray if Hezekiah were evil in God's sight. Are Christians to pray based on our own merits before God? Certainly, God does not hear the wicked, but does he listen to Christians because they are righteous through their own actions? The Bible is consistent in its statement that what pleases God is faith, that is, trust in him as the true God. This trust tends to be exhibited in obedience to God's commands and rejection of false gods. This is exactly what was true in Hezekiah's life. We can say, then, that our merit before God comes from faith in Christ—true God and true man—rather than our own righteousness. So, when we pray, it is not our personal piety that causes God to listen as such, but growing personal piety is a consequence of trust in Christ.

Secondly, if Hezekiah had died as God said he would instead of living another fifteen years, then his son Manasseh would not have been born.

Manasseh was a terribly wicked king and undid all the good his father did before him (2 Kgs 21:1–9). The consequence of his evil and the evil he led Judah to do was that God judged them severely. It might have been better for Hezekiah to bow to the sovereignty of God and accept his death. Yet, we cannot know what would have happened if he had died and Manasseh had not been born. Trying to figure out the possible consequences of the prayers we pray can become an intolerable burden. Only God has knowledge of the future, and he alone is able to answer our prayers. Instead of worrying about such things, it is best to pray in faith, trusting that God will say No if the consequences of our prayer are outside his sovereign will.

Jehoshaphat's Weakness and His Strength

We have met the second king with a powerful prayer life previously. Jehoshaphat was a good king, who sought God and was devoted to him (2 Chr 17:3–6). We have already seen how Jehoshaphat asked for a prophet so he could inquire of the LORD before going into battle (1 Kgs 22:7) and when there was a serious problem on the way to battle (2 Kgs 3:11). However, he had an issue that needed to be addressed in his life. Jehoshaphat's problem was that he allied himself with Ahab by marriage (2 Chr 18:1). Consequently, Jehoshaphat tended to ally himself with the king of Israel in battle (see 1 Kgs 22; 2 Chr 18; 2 Kgs 3). This resulted in a rebuke from the prophet Jehu son of Hanani (2 Chr 19:1–3). Heed the warning that even a godly king, who prayed and sought God, could have a weakness. In this case, the weakness was being unequally yoked with a godless king of Israel. If we want our prayer lives to improve, then asking deep questions about bad influences in our lives may make the difference between good and best.

Nonetheless, Jehoshaphat showed himself to be a man of prayer when the Moabites, Ammonites and Meunites came as a horde to battle against Judah. This large army unsurprisingly caused Jehoshaphat to be afraid. Instead of panicking or seeking an ally to help him, Jehoshaphat determined to seek the LORD. He had the whole of Judah fast with him. Many people came from the towns of Judah to Jerusalem to seek God's help (2 Chr 20:1–4). The situation which faced Judah did not merely affect the king, but the whole nation. Jehoshaphat acted like a godly leader and not only prayed and fasted himself but led others to do so as well. The goal of Christian leadership is discipleship of the people over whom the leader is given responsibility. It may be that the LORD would have given Jehoshaphat victory based on his prayer alone. However, in contradistinction to those wicked kings who led the people into idol worship, Jehoshaphat led the people into deeper trust in the LORD. He encouraged the prayer lives of the people.

> And Jehoshaphat stood in the assembly of Judah and Jerusalem, in the house of the LORD, before the new court, and said, "O LORD, God of our fathers, are you not God in heaven? You rule over all the kingdoms of the nations. In your hand are power and might, so that none is able to withstand you. Did you not, our God, drive out the inhabitants of this land before your people Israel, and give it forever to the descendants of Abraham your friend? And they have lived in it and have built for you in it a sanctuary for your name, saying, 'If disaster comes upon us, the sword, judgement, or pestilence, or famine, we will stand before this house and before you—for your name is in this house—and cry out to you in our affliction, and you will hear and save.' And now behold, the men of Ammon and Moab and Mount Seir, whom you would not let Israel invade when they came from the land of Egypt, and whom they avoided and did not destroy—behold, they reward us by coming to drive us out of your possession, which you have given us

to inherit. O our God, will you not execute judgement on them? For we are powerless against this great horde that is coming against us. We do not know what to do, but our eyes are on you." (2 Chr 20:5–12)

Jehoshaphat's prayer began with a reminder of who God is. He is the God of Israel's fathers, that is, God of the patriarchs, to whom God gave great promises. This, then, was a shorthand way of speaking of God as the one who promised to bless the nation and a reminder that God had not changed, nor had his word. He is God in heaven and ruler of nations on earth. Being the God in heaven, he must be greater than any armies which come against Judah. Indeed, he is, because he is the sovereign ruler, not just of Judah but even of those nations who do not worship him. There were further reminders in this prayer of what God had done in the past for Israel. He drove out the peoples of the land and gave the land to Israel. This, as we know, involved many battles for Israel, but they were battles in which the victory came from God. The land on which Jehoshaphat stood belonged to the people of God because of God's promise. Thus, they could ask for help to retain the land. The last reminder was of God's promise to Solomon when he prayed the great prayer of dedication for the temple. When God's people prayed towards the temple, he would hear and save.

It is hardly necessary for God to be reminded of who he is, but biblical prayers often begin this way. Not only did it remind the person praying of the God they served, but reminding God of his nature, character and promises was the foundation of the request which followed. This is always a good beginning to our prayer. God does not answer because of who we are, or because we have something in us which would make him listen. Rather, he hears because he has promised to do so for the sake of his Son, Jesus Christ (John 15:16; 16:23, 27). We can rely on God remaining faithful to himself and his word. Reminding God of these things at the beginning of our prayer also serves to remind us of truth and this encourages and grows faith. Faith is a necessary part of prayer (Heb 11:6).

After having reminded God of all these things, Jehoshaphat then got down to the issue in front of him, a huge invading army. Jehoshaphat argued that the people coming to invade Israel had no cause to be doing so. When Israel came from Egypt, the Israelites did not invade any of these nations because God would not allow them to do so. Yet these same people who Israel treated well were now threatening Judah. The land of Judah was land given by God as an inheritance to his people and no one had the right to take it away. "O our God, will you not execute judgement on them?" This was primarily an appeal to God's justice. This appeal to God's justice was repeated elsewhere in the prayers of Old Testament saints, beginning with Abraham asking, "Shall not the Judge of all the earth do what is just?" (Gen 18:25c).

Finally, Jehoshaphat confessed how weak and powerless the small nation of Judah was against three invading hordes. He pleaded with God to help them. He had no strategy to defeat the enemy but only looked to his God, whom he trusted. The solution which the LORD provided was not one which we might expect. The LORD told them to take a stand, but they would not need to fight the battle. Instead, Jehoshaphat appointed singers to praise God. "And when they began to sing and praise, the LORD set an ambush against the men of Ammon, Moab, and Mount Seir, who had come against Judah, so that they were routed" (2 Chr 20:22). The focus of Jehoshaphat's prayer was such that the LORD chose to display his glory by winning the battle on behalf of his people.

"We do not know what to do, but our eyes are on you" is a prayer I have prayed many times. How often we are confronted with situations that have no solution, naturally speaking? The LORD does unexpected things in response to this prayer. God does not always do the same thing to bring about deliverance. For David, he sometimes gave battle plans (2 Sam 5:24) and for Gideon he gave a ruse to discombobulate the enemy (Judg 7:16, 20). There is no reason to believe that singing praise will always bring victory, any more than making a bronze snake (see Num 21:9) will heal all illnesses. The prayer is one of trust that the LORD is able to do far more than we can ask or imagine (Eph 3:20). Leave it up to him to do what he sees fit in the situation.

Josiah: The Last Good King

The final good king, Josiah, was only recorded as praying once, yet he sought the LORD his whole life. "And he did what was right in the eyes of the LORD and walked in all the way of David his father, and he did not turn aside to the right or to the left" (2 Kgs 22:2). Like his ancestor David, Josiah focused his attention on things which would please God. He repaired the temple, and in doing so the book of the law was found. When the book was read the king was deeply grieved and concerned, and he ordered the priest and his attendants (2 Kgs 22:3–12), "Go, inquire of the LORD for me, and for the people, and for all Judah, concerning the words of this book that has been found. For great is the wrath of the LORD that is kindled against us, because our fathers have not obeyed the words of this book, to do according to all that is written concerning us" (2 Kgs 22:13).

In contrast to some inquiries to the LORD by earlier kings, this inquiry went to the prophet Huldah, who gave Josiah an answer from God. The LORD's answer was not comforting. He was angry with his people for their idol worship and would bring judgement according to what was written in the book of the law. But there was some good news for Josiah himself because he was contrite and humbled himself when he heard the words of the law. That good news was that Josiah would die and be buried in peace before the dreadful judgement would arrive (2 Kgs 22:14–20).

Josiah was zealous in his repentance. He read the book of the law to the people and renewed the covenant. He rid the land of all the detestable idols worshipped there, including those at Bethel in the north. Then he celebrated the Passover and removed the mediums and spiritists from the land. This, however, was not enough; the LORD was still angry. Josiah died in battle at age thirty-nine (2 Kgs 23:1–29).

What are we to make of this king, who was so zealous for the LORD and yet died so young? God was pleased with the zeal of Josiah. We see only one recorded prayer of Josiah and even that was not prayed directly to God, but rather through the prophet. Josiah had a poor example in his evil, idolatrous father (2 Kgs 21:19). Possibly, Josiah was not instructed sufficiently in prayer for his prayer life to be better. The task of priests was to instruct people, including the king, in the law (Lev 10:10–11; 2 Kgs 17:13; 2 Kgs 17:27; 2 Chr 35:3). It is evident that since the book of the law was lost, they had not been conducting this sacred duty. Josiah's desire was for God and yet he did not have a long life in which to grow closer to God. He worshipped God according to his knowledge of God and prayed in this way also. Since Josiah was a good king, no doubt he would have developed a richer prayer life if he had both knowledge and time.

Conclusion

This selection of good kings and their prayers offer us some examples for Christian leaders. Kings of Israel had great privileges but also great responsibility. The better kings, like Hezekiah, Jehoshaphat and Josiah, were concerned with leading the nation in their care to trust in the LORD. They prayed accordingly. Their prayers exalted the LORD and expressed faith in him as the true God. In the case of Jehoshaphat, prayer was not restricted to the king but involved the whole nation. Josiah's desire was to see the nation repent of sin and idol worship and return to full obedience to God's law. Christian leaders can learn from these examples. Pray for those in the flock which you shepherd so that they will trust in the living God. Provide examples of public prayer that focus on who God is and what he has done. Teach people to pray kingdom prayers, prayers which seek God's glory. Pray that your congregation loves God's word and is obedient to him. All these will help your church to grow in faith and also grow better prayer lives.

Reflection Questions / Journal Prompts

1. Are there inappropriate influences in your life that are hindering your prayer life?
2. If you are a Christian leader of any kind (including a parent), in what ways are you encouraging and strengthening the prayer lives of people whom you are called to lead?
3. How are you teaching others to pray in more biblical ways?
4. Remind yourself of God's redemptive acts on behalf of his people, both in Old Testament and New Testament. Praise him for these.

Job's Prayers: Expressing Pain in Prayer

The story of Job, at least in outline, is familiar to many. The patience of Job is considered an example for Christians (Jas 5:11). His prayer life can also provide some instruction for believers. Job's trials were extreme, and his prayers changed as the book progressed. He began with praise, moved into lament, pleaded for God to listen to him, repented when confronted with God's power, and finally prayed for his misguided friends.

Job's Life Was Turned Upside Down

Job was a good man, a pious man, who sought to please God in his life. God blessed Job greatly. But one day, he was struck down with disaster after disaster. All of his ten children died on one day. On the same day, his property was ruined (Job 1:1–19). Job's response to this series of disasters was worship of God. "Then Job arose and tore his robe and shaved his head and fell on the ground and worshipped. And he said, 'Naked I came from my mother's womb, and naked shall I return. The LORD gave, and the LORD has taken away; blessed be the name of the LORD'" (Job 1:20–21).

All Job had left was his wife and his health, but soon his health was also taken from him (Job 2:1–8). "Then his wife said to him, 'Do you still hold fast your integrity? Curse God and die.' But he said to her, 'You speak as one of the foolish women would speak. Shall we receive good from God, and shall we not receive evil?' In all this Job did not sin with his lips" (Job 2:9–10). The default for Job was to take everything to God and to give God praise. He refused to give in to the impulses of his foolish wife. His trust in God was demonstrated in what he prayed and what he refused to pray.

Job Lamented

Job made a lot of speeches in the book. Many were directed at his friends and their wrong understanding of his situation. However, there were some speeches directed at God himself. Job's prayers were full of his frustration and sorrow for his situation, which he knew was undeserved. He lamented, "Remember that my life is a breath; my eye will never again see good" (Job 7:7). The ESV does not make clear who this was directed towards, but the NIV adds "Oh God", making this statement a prayer. Without doubt, the remainder of Job's speech in Job 7 was directed at God.

> "Therefore I will not restrain my mouth; I will speak in the anguish of my spirit; I will complain in the bitterness of my soul. Am I the sea, or a sea monster, that you set a guard over me? When I say, 'My bed will comfort me, my couch will ease my complaint,' then you scare me with dreams and terrify me with visions, so that I would choose strangling and death rather than my bones. I loathe my life; I would not live forever. Leave me alone, for my days are a breath. What is man, that you make so much of him, and that you set your heart on him, visit him every morning and test him every moment? How long will you not look away from me, nor leave me alone till I swallow my spit? If I sin, what do I do to you, you watcher of mankind? Why have you made me your mark? Why have I become a burden to you? Why do you not pardon my transgression and take away my iniquity? For now I shall lie in the earth; you will seek me, but I shall not be." (Job 7:11–21)

Job's raw emotion here was directed towards God. He wanted to know why God was so intently focused on his life and thereby caused his intense misery. He wanted God to leave him alone for a time instead of testing him continually. The prayer itself was very intense. It seemed almost blasphemous in its questions. How are we to read this? There is a kind of psalm called a lament psalm, in which the psalmist gives voice to a complaint to God. Usually, lament psalms have statements of faith and praise in them, although these may come at the end. Generally, they contain some sort of resolution of the complaint (see *Pain: A Biblical Perspective*[1] for more details about lament). Job offered no praise and there was no resolution of his complaint at this point of the book. All we are left with is the pain of his heart expressed in prayer.

This is not the only prayer of this kind in the book. We can gain some perspective of how God felt about Job's prayers at the end of the book. For now, let's look at what else Job prayed.

Job understood that God is great and that his power is beyond ours in ways that dwarf anything we could do. God is wiser than all humans. He made the earth and the stars in the heavens. His wonders are beyond understanding. He is not visible to us. None can stop him. Job wanted God to go to court with him. Yet he realized that there is no way to dispute with God. God was able to crush Job, and he is completely just so that he can pronounce even the innocent guilty. Job was mortal and had already been found guilty (Job 9:1–31). Therefore, Job again lamented: "For he is not a man, as I am, that I might answer him, that we should come to trial together. There is no arbiter between us, who might lay his hand on us both. Let him take his rod away from me, and let not dread of him terrify me. Then I would speak without fear of him, for I am not so in myself" (Job 9:32–35). This was not a prayer as such. But it expressed Job's desire to find a mediator so that he could bring his dispute to God successfully. The only mediator we can ever need is the Lord Jesus (1 Tim 2:5), although Job did not know this, living long before the incarnation.

---

1. *https://www.smashwords.com/books/view/1115430*

Job's renewed prayer of lament spans the whole of Job 10. He cried out, "I loathe my life; I will give free utterance to my complaint; I will speak in the bitterness of my soul" (Job 10:1). Thus began another free expression of bitterness directed towards God. Job asked God to stop opposing him. He wanted to know whether God actually despised what he had created. Is God like a man that he would want to look for Job's sins? Job accused God of making him and then destroying him: turned from clay to dust, poured out like milk and curdled. At this point, Job observed that God created him carefully, gave him life and love, and preserved his spirit. But then he went back to accusing God of working against him. He insisted that guilt or innocence don't seem to make any difference before God because God was hunting him like a lion and bringing an army against him (Job 10:2–17). Then there were final dreadful questions:

> "Why did you bring me out from the womb? Would that I had died before any eye had seen me and were as though I had not been, carried from the womb to the grave. Are not my days few? Then cease, and leave me alone, that I may find a little cheer before I go—and I shall not return—to the land of darkness and deep shadow, the land of gloom like thick darkness, like deep shadow without any order, where light is as thick darkness." (Job 10:18–22)

Job did not hold back his painful emotions in this prayer. It contained bitter statements about God's treatment of Job, questions about why these things were happening, and an expression of Job's deep depression. At the same time, his prayer had features somewhat similar to prayers we have looked at earlier. He appealed to the character of God and his motivation, to the distinction between humanity and God, to God's knowledge of truth, to the fact that God made Job, and to God's love. These different elements of the way Job understood God were not disconnected in this prayer. They were, for Job, of a piece. Job was trying to reconcile what he believed about God's justice with his own experience, which at that point was awful.

Job desired a meeting with God to discuss his sins and what had happened to him. He boldly asked, "Only grant me two things, then I will not hide myself from your face: withdraw your hand far from me, and let not dread of you terrify me. Then call, and I will answer; or let me speak, and you reply to me" (Job 13:20–22). He continued in this vein, asking that God make his sin known, demanding answers as to why God was his enemy, an enemy who frightened him and brought all manner of bitterness against him (Job 13:23–28). In praying this prayer, Job assumed that God is the author of both good and bad. Job was perhaps too bold, as we will see later. But there was no "smiting" by God here, as people often imagine will happen when someone prays like this.

Job's depression did not let up. He asked God to hide him in the grave until God's wrath had come to an end. There, Job could wait until God called him to life again. That way Job's sins would be covered, and God would not be so vigilant in looking for them (Job 14:13–17). Then his words to God became more bitter than previously. "I cry to you for help and you do not answer me; I stand, and you only look at me. You have turned cruel to me; with the might of your hand you persecute me. You lift me up on the wind; you make me ride on it, and you toss me about in the roar of the storm. For I know that you will bring me to death and to the house appointed for all living" (Job 30:20–23). These were the words of a man who had no idea why God had afflicted him and why God did not answer his pleas for mercy and relief. We hope that there will be some answers for Job later in the book, but there are not. He never received any indication of what the reader knows, that Satan was responsible for his ordeal, that God was using his affliction to show Job's faithfulness to God even in the absence of blessing.

God Spoke to Job

However, God did answer Job's request for a meeting. In the final chapters of the book, God appeared to Job. Job 30–41 is a long soliloquy by the LORD. The arguments God used in this speech were mainly about the wonders of creation that only God has made and only he controls and understands. It was written in the form of many rhetorical questions. In the middle of this, Job responded to the LORD. "And the LORD said to Job: 'Shall a faultfinder contend with the Almighty? He who argues with God, let him answer it.' Then Job answered the LORD and said: 'Behold, I am of small account; what shall I answer you? I lay my hand on my mouth. I have spoken once, and I will not answer; twice, but I will proceed no further'" (Job 40:1–5). For all his boldness in prayer prior to this, Job became humble and speechless. This was not the answer that Job imagined to his prayers. He could not but be quiet in the face of the Almighty himself. Even though this long speech from God did not explain anything to Job, it demonstrated that, by virtue of who he is in relation to the world, God was not obligated to provide Job (or anyone else for that matter) with the answers to Job's questions.

At the end of the book, several things happened. First of all, Job prayed a prayer of wonder and repentance in the face of what he had seen of God close up.

> Then Job answered the LORD and said: "I know that you can do all things, and that no purpose of yours can be thwarted. 'Who is this that hides counsel without knowledge?' Therefore I have uttered what I did not understand, things too wonderful for me, which I did not know. 'Hear, and I will speak; I will question you, and you make it known to me.' I had heard of you by the hearing of

the ear, but now my eye sees you; therefore I despise myself, and repent in dust and ashes." (Job 42:1–6)

Meeting God humbled Job profoundly. By this point, he had lost all of his bravado.

Humility before God is a good start in prayer. We acknowledge that God knows all, and we know very little. We do not know his plans. This is a far better place to begin than with the arrogant kinds of declarations which demand that God do what we say. Genuine experience of God's presence will bring this kind of humility in a way that nothing else can. It is unlikely that any of us will experience the kind of encounter with God that Job did. We are never promised such a thing. What we can do is to get to know God through his word to us. This will not bring lasting change to our hearts if we do not first realise that we can know God only through Christ. But as people in Christ, we can grow in our relationship with God as we seek him, open the Bible, learn the truth about God, and take to heart this truth. This will lead to humility, faith and repentance.

Throughout the book of Job, Job's friends spent endless hours trying to get Job to see that his problems were because of his sins, when Job knew all along that this was not the case. The reader knows Job was innocent because the beginning and end of the book tell us what God thought of Job. The narrator tells us that Job "was blameless and upright, one who feared God and turned away from evil" (Job 1:1b). God was also of that opinion (Job 1:8; 2:3). In the closing passage of the book, we see what God thought of Job in comparison to Job's friends.

> After the LORD had spoken these words to Job, the LORD said to Eliphaz the Temanite: "My anger burns against you and against your two friends, for you have not spoken of me what is right, as my servant Job has. Now therefore take

> seven bulls and seven rams and go to my servant Job and offer up a burnt offering for yourselves. And my servant Job shall pray for you, for I will accept his prayer not to deal with you according to your folly. For you have not spoken of me what is right, as my servant Job has." So Eliphaz the Temanite and Bildad the Shuhite and Zophar the Naamathite went and did what the LORD had told them, and the LORD accepted Job's prayer. (Job 42:7–9)

Job was effectively declared righteous by God in this passage. The friends were wrong in their understanding of God. Their theology was wrong, and God was not pleased with it. God asked for a sacrifice for their sin. He also asked that Job pray for the friends, which Job did, and it was accepted by God. It should not surprise us that God accepted Job's prayer when he had commanded that Job pray. In praying for the friends, Job was acting as a prophet (compare Abraham and Abimelech in Gen 20:4–18), and in offering sacrifices, Job acted like a priest. It is the prayer of a righteous man that God accepts, not that of the wicked (see Prov 15:29; Jas 5:16; 1 Pet 3:12).

Conclusion

God's affirmation of Job's righteousness and of Job's words at the end of the book give us some perspective on Job's prayers in the middle of the book. The raw emotion of those prayers, even the words Job spoke accusing God, were not condemned by God. God did not say that Job should not have prayed these things. He was not angry with Job as such. But the truth is that Job prayed without knowledge of God's plans, forgetting that God is wiser than we could ever be. Human beings, no matter how righteous in the sight of God, are still mortal beings. We cannot compare to God at all. Yet, there are times when letting out our raw emotions in prayer, as long as this is done in humility and faith, is appropriate and acceptable to God. The trick is always the balance of faith, humility and boldness.

Reflection Questions / Journal Prompts

1. Reflect on a difficult experience in your life. What was your initial reaction to this experience? How did it impact your trust in God?
2. During this difficult time, how did you express your emotions to God in prayer?
3. In what ways does the story of Job change your understanding of difficult experiences?
4. Consider the sovereignty of God over your life and thank him regardless of whether your experience is good or bad right now.

Isaiah: A Theology of Prayer

In the book of Isaiah, there are less prayers of the prophet and more explicit theology regarding prayer. There is a great deal to say about prayer that the LORD would not hear. The people were idol worshippers, and injustice was rampant. The LORD was angry, and judgement was coming soon. And yet, there was hope for a future when even the nations outside Israel would worship the true God, God would transform Israel, and he would hear them even before they call to him.

God Does Not Listen to the Wicked

The first oracle of Isaiah was a poetic rebuke of Judah because they did not know their own God. The nation had forsaken God and rebelled against him. Judgement was coming but they did not turn back. The sacrifices which were offered to God were not pleasing to him. He was angry with those who came to the temple and with all the feasts they celebrated. The worship of Israel was but a burden to the LORD (Isa 1:2–14; see also Amos 5:21–27). This was the backdrop to God's view of their prayers. "When you spread out your hands, I will hide my eyes from you; even though you make many prayers, I will not listen; your hands are full of blood" (Isa 1:15).

All the "worship" of God that went on the temple was worthless to God, even though the sacrifices and offerings were actually prescribed by him. The sacrificial system was set up so that the people of Israel could draw near to God, and he could be present in their midst (Exod 25:8; Num 5:3; 14:14; 35:34). However, just because these things were instituted by God did not mean that God would automatically accept those sacrifices. At the time Isaiah prophesied, people were taking for granted the idea that doing the religious things correctly was enough. But God is concerned with more than just outward rituals.

The LORD commanded the people to clean themselves up and wash away their evil deeds. They had to learn how to act justly, correct oppression and look after widows and orphans (Isa 1:16–17). Injustice was standing in the way of God accepting their worship and hearing their prayers. Jerusalem was no longer a place of justice but instead a city full of murderers, thieves, corruption and exploitation of the poor (Isa 1:21–23). The offer of forgiveness and restoration was open if they chose to repent and turn back to God, but the threat of judgement hung over them if they did not return (Isa 1:18–20). The final chapter of 2 Kgs informs us that judgement did come to Judah and they were carried off to exile in Babylon (2 Kgs 25).

The idea that God does not listen to the prayers of the wicked is expanded upon in Isa 58–59. The people of Judah were rebellious against God. The LORD declared,

> "Yet they seek me daily and delight to know my ways, as if they were a nation that did righteousness and did not forsake the judgement of their God; they ask of me righteous judgements; they delight to draw near to God. 'Why have we fasted, and you see it not? Why have we humbled ourselves, and you take no knowledge of it?' Behold, in the day of your fast you seek your own pleasure, and oppress all your workers. Behold, you fast only to quarrel and to fight and to hit with a wicked fist. Fasting like yours this day will not make your voice to be heard on high."
> (Isa 58:2–4)

These people had done all you might expect a nation to do in order to be heard by God. They sought God and said how much they wanted to know his ways. They fasted and prayed. Yet it was all a sham. In reality, no one wanted to know God; they wanted merely to look good on the outside, to appear to be pious and religious. They fasted and looked humble but only for show. It was a strange kind of fast, when on the day of the fast people looked for pleasure. The religious life was only a façade, a fake outer shell. However, God was not fooled by such things. He desires a heart that genuinely seeks to please him. This involves being just: eschewing violence, treating workers fairly, stopping oppression, feeding the hungry, clothing the naked, helping the poor and caring for your own family (Isa 58:4–7). "Then you shall call, and the LORD will answer; you shall cry, and he will say, 'Here I am.' If you take away the yoke from your midst, the pointing of the finger, and speaking wickedness" (Isa 58:9).

Isaiah 59 repeats these ideas. "Behold, the LORD's hand is not shortened, that it cannot save, or his ear dull, that it cannot hear; but your iniquities have made a separation between you and your God, and your sins have hidden his face from you so that he does not hear. For your hands are defiled with blood and your fingers with iniquity; your lips have spoken lies; your tongue mutters wickedness" (Isa 59:1–3). The LORD was not reluctant to save his people or unwilling to listen. He is able to save, able to answer them if they called to him. But sin is a huge problem. Surely a holy and just God does not hear the people who rebel against him and who live like the godless—lying, cheating and perpetrating violence. Prayer is a part of relationship with the true God. But that relationship is broken by sin, rendering prayer no longer effective.

Is it true that God does not hear prayer if we harbour sin? In the above case, this was absolutely true. God's relationship with Israel was set out in the form of a covenant, in which God stipulated how they were to live and their obligations to him (see the book of Deuteronomy). For his part, this covenant was established when the LORD redeemed

Israel from slavery in Egypt. God did not bless those who broke his covenant. The expectation of the wicked could only be judgement, even if God often showed them mercy for a time. But what about Christians? Are we not forgiven of all our sins in Christ? Is not our righteousness the righteousness of Christ?

The answer to that question is more complex that a simple Yes or No. Faith in Christ is what God requires of us in order for us to be righteous in his sight. Faith in Christ and not obedience to the law is the way to salvation (Rom 3:21–31). There is no way to be saved through works (Gal 2:16). We can come to God in prayer because of Jesus (Eph 2:18). Does this mean that I can sin now to my heart's content and God will still hear me? It would be foolish to think that Christians never sin (1 John 1:8), but sin should not make our hearts content. It should grieve us because we know it does not please God. In fact, to be in habitual sin is to be outside the kingdom of God (1 Cor 6:9–10; Gal 5:21). God disciplines his children (Heb 12:6, 10) and therefore, if, as a Christian, you are sinning in a way similar to the above then you might expect the discipline of God would include not answering when you pray. But remember, if you are in habitual sin, it is not too late for repentance.

God Does Not Listen to Idolators

The second major reason why God did not answer prayer for Judah was idolatry. The problem of idol worship comes up repeatedly in the prophetic books. It was a central issue that resulted in God's judgement upon both Israel and Judah and had them sent into exile. The LORD alone is God (Exod 34:14; Deut 4:35; 1 Kgs 8:60) and he does not share his glory with others (Isa 48:11). He would not answer prayer if the people sought out idols instead of the living God.

The LORD is truly God, but idols are constructed by people. Isaiah described the way a craftsman builds an idol from the same wood he uses to make a fire. The fire keeps him warm, but he bows down to the idol, worships it and prays to it, saying, "Deliver me for you are my god!" (Isa 44:12–17). Both the idol and those who worship it are blind, unable to see and understand (Isa 44:18). How could a block of wood save anyone? How could an idol constructed by a human being ever answer prayer. As Christians, we must take care that we do not carelessly construct idols out of ordinary things and put them in the place of God. That is, do not rely on what cannot be relied upon.

The subject of idols comes up many times in Isaiah. Idol worship in Judah involved immoral sexual practices, sacrificing children as well as wine and grain offerings. This was a manifestation of their rebellion against the LORD, the God of Israel. He was against them because of this (Isa 57:3–12). He says, "When you cry out, let your collection of idols deliver you! The wind will carry them all off, a breath will take them away. But he who takes refuge in me shall possess the land and shall inherit my holy mountain" (Isa 57:13). The idolatrous people of Judah put a lot of effort into pleasing their useless idols. They would soon be in hot water because of their sin; the Babylonians were coming to execute God's judgement. And God mocked them by inviting them to get help from their idols.

Isaiah warned, "And when they say to you, 'Inquire of the mediums and the necromancers who chirp and mutter,' should not a people inquire of their God? Should they inquire of the dead on behalf of the living? To the teaching and to the testimony! If they will not speak according to this word, it is because they have no dawn" (Isa 8:19–20). A medium is a go-between who connects people with spirits, and a necromancer speaks to the dead. Inquiring of these is not consulting an idol but it is certainly not consulting God himself. All spirituality is not equal in any sense. When a person seeks wisdom from the dead instead of from the LORD, this is not genuine prayer. If you want wisdom, then go to God's written word—"to the teaching and to the testimony". If you want help, go to God in prayer. Even supposing the mediums and necromancers could genuinely speak to the dead, being dead does not make a person wise or able to answer prayer. That is a delusion. In reality, the dead have nothing to offer.

When Isaiah was given a prophecy against Egypt, part of what the LORD would do to bring defeat upon Egypt is this: "I will confound their counsel; and they will inquire of the idols and the sorcerers, and the mediums and the necromancers" (Isa 19:3b). In this context there was nothing helpful about this statement. It was instead a curse. With nothing to rely on except these useless means of getting counsel for battle, the Egyptians would lose the battle against the oppressor. There is never any value to be had from these false forms of prayer because those entities people pray to have no power to answer or help.

Another useless form of prayer involves turning for help to others instead of turning to God for help. "Woe to those who go down to Egypt for help and rely on horses, who trust in chariots because they are many and in horsemen because they are very strong, but do not look to the Holy One of Israel or consult the LORD!" (Isa 31:1). The problem here was not that somewhere in Israel people were helping other people, something which we are called to do for our fellow believers and in fact for other people who are not Christians. Rather this was a matter of rebelling against God and ousting him from his rightful place as the defender of his people (Isa 30:1–5). Egypt had a particular relationship to Israel. Israel was rescued by God from slavery in Egypt and yet they regularly wanted to go back there, even from the beginning (Exod 17:3; Num 11:5, 18, 20; 14:2–4).

The Egyptians were not gods, yet the people of Judah wanted their help as if they were that powerful (Isa 31:3). God called the people to repent of their sinful dependence on Egypt and turn back to him. "Turn to him from whom people have deeply revolted, O children of Israel. For in that day everyone shall cast away his idols of silver and his idols of gold, which your hands have sinfully made for you" (Isa 31:6–7). This passage implies that it was not merely to humans that the people of Judah turned but also to idols, perhaps to the false gods of Egypt, those which the God of Israel had judged in the exodus (Exod 12:12). Rejecting idols is a good thing, because it would mean that Israel had turned back to trust in the true God.

On the other hand, there were religious people whose religion was nothing but hypocrisy. They made up their own laws and pretended that this honoured God. "And the Lord said: 'Because this people draw near with their mouth and honour me with their lips, while their hearts are far from me, and their fear of me is a commandment taught by men'" (Isa 29:13). These were religious people, people who sounded and looked good on the outside. I wonder if they "said their prayers" like pious people, expecting that God would also be impressed by their religiosity. God is impressed only by a heart that desires to obey him, not by those who are only outwardly righteous. Jesus is the only one who was fully obedient to God from a right heart. However, we may imitate him by dropping the pretence and speaking what is true when we pray.

Hope For Change

Despite Isaiah's many prophecies of judgement against the people of Judah, and the condemnation of the Egyptians, there is a day coming when the LORD himself will transform people, including the Egyptians. The LORD will turn the Egyptians into those who call upon him and worship him. "And the LORD will strike Egypt, striking and healing, and they will return to the LORD, and he will listen to their pleas for mercy and heal them" (Isa 19:22). It is not just the Egyptians who will be heard by the LORD. He says to the people of Judah, "For a people shall dwell in Zion, in Jerusalem; you shall weep no more. He will surely be gracious to you at the sound of your cry. As soon as he hears it, he answers you" (Isa 30:19). This will be the result of God's work within the people. They will desecrate their idols and rid the land of them (Isa 30:22).

Because this transformation had not yet happened, Isaiah prayed for it to happen. "O LORD, why do you make us wander from your ways and harden our heart, so that we fear you not? Return for the sake of your servants, the tribes of your heritage" (Isa 63:17). This prayer acknowledged that even human sinfulness is within the sovereignty of God. It requires a work of God in the human heart to change a person into a godly human being. This is exactly what happens when a person is united with Christ through faith. God transforms the heart (Ezek 36:26).

Close to the end of Isaiah, the people were still in exile and wanted to see God move to change their situation. Isaiah prayed for God to do awesome things as he had done in the past. He asked for God to come down from heaven and make the mountains tremble and the nations to be afraid before the face of God. He reminded God of the awesome deeds done in the past. The God of Israel is the only God who acts on behalf of those who wait for him. He helps them and opposes those who sin against him. Isaiah confessed that all the people were unclean before God (Isa 64:1–6). "There is no one who calls upon your name, who rouses himself to take hold of you; for you have hidden your face from us, and have made us melt in the hand of our iniquities" (Isa 64:7). The people did not pray because they believed God was angry and would not listen. Hence Isaiah pleaded on the basis that they were the people of God. The cities of Judah were in ruin as was the temple. Therefore, he asked that God would not stay silent but act on behalf of his people (Isa 64:8–12).

Something happened when the people went into exile. The first half of Isaiah was written to the people before the exile and it focused on their sin, calling them to repentance. They did not repent, and the Babylonians came; God used the wicked nation of Babylon to punish his people for their sins. But the second half of Isaiah was written to people in exile, hoping to be able to return home. The prayers of people in exile were different from those before the exile (I will examine this further in a later chapter). There was more humility because the people had realised that they were sinners, who deserved their punishment. The reality of sin was not a theory but one which people had come to understand as applicable to each of them. In this prayer, Isaiah remembered what he knew God is like. He wanted to see God do great things again. The call for God to act was a plea for mercy rather than a demand. It was a cry for forgiveness and restoration.

The answer to this prayer was that the people of Judah had continually rejected the God who called to them to hear him. They offered sacrifices to idols, ate unclean animals, and would have nothing to do with the true God. He would punish them as they deserved (Isa 65:1–7). However, there was also a promise of mercy. There would be a remnant, who would inherit the land, namely, those who seek their God (Isa 65:8–10). There would be a distinction between those who persist in running after false gods and do not answer when the LORD calls and the servants of the LORD. The servants of God will eat, drink and have joy, and God will give them a new name (Isa 65:11–16). Then there will be none who pray to idols. "So that he who blesses himself in the land shall bless himself by the God of truth, and he who takes an oath in the land shall swear by the God of truth; because the former troubles are forgotten and are hidden from my eyes" (Isa 65:16). There will be new heavens and a new earth. Part of the blessing of this eschatological transformation of the world will be that God will hear prayer. God promises, "Before they call I will answer; while they are yet speaking I will hear" (Isa 65:24).

Conclusion

Human beings, not just the people of Israel and Judah, are idol worshippers by nature. We don't seek God, even if sometimes people seek to look pious with their religious actions. We wonder why God does not give us what we want (compare Jas 4:2–3), but at the same time humans think it is acceptable to look after ourselves with no concern for the vulnerable, the weak and the poor. The story of prayer in the wrong way to the wrong gods is our story. But there is hope in Christ. God has promised that he will hear his people. Jesus was the only human who ever fully loved God and other people. Therefore, God always answered Jesus. His righteousness becomes ours when we trust him. This righteousness is more than theoretical. The Holy Spirit sanctifies and transforms God's people, often using suffering in the process. Ultimately, there will be a new heaven and new earth in which God will be so near that he will answer us before we call.

Reflection Questions / Journal Prompts

1. God listens to the prayers of Christians because of the righteousness of Christ. However, it is right to repent of our sin. Ask the Holy Spirit to reveal sin to you.
2. It is easy to slip into trusting in something instead of putting trust in God. Consider what you turn to when in trouble. Is it the true God or something you use for a coping mechanism?
3. Can you think of times when you simply go through the motions of prayer without true love of God?
4. Praise God that he has given Christian believers a new heart and a new spirit (Ezek 36:26; Jer 31:33).

Jeremiah: A Praying Prophet

———

Prayer features frequently in the book of Jeremiah. Jeremiah both prays and is commanded not to pray. He repeatedly complains to the LORD about his life and his calling. Other people pray in a myriad of wrong ways. They treat the LORD like a buddy, presume upon his deliverance, trust in their prayer formula, and ask when they never intend to obey the answer. Despite the inevitability of judgement, there are signs of hope for a future with God. Because Jeremiah contains a lot of prayers, this chapter has several parts to it, and each has its own set of reflection questions.

Part 1

The People Reaped What They Sowed

AS WITH THE PROPHECIES of Isaiah, a central issue with unanswered prayer was that the people of Judah rebelled against the LORD and ran after idols (Jer 2:4–26). Kings, priests and prophets were among those "who say to a tree, 'You are my father,' and to a stone, 'You gave me birth.' For they have turned their back to me, and not their face. But in the time of their trouble they say, 'Arise and save us!' But where are your gods that you made for yourself? Let them arise, if they can save you, in your time of trouble; for as many as your cities are your gods, O Judah" (Jer 2:27–28). Since the people had gone off after foreign gods, worthless idols, the living God mocked them when they asked him for help. We cannot have it both ways. Either we worship worthless idols, who are unable to help in times of trouble, or we worship the God who made heaven and earth. God is not mocked.

You reap what you sow (see Gal 6:7). In this case, if your life is set on pursuing idols, God will not answer you when you are in trouble.

The people of Judah had a flippant attitude towards the LORD. Their desire for idols and for doing wickedness was insatiable. They had no shame about such sinful behaviour (Jer 3:1–3). Yet they still believed that they could come to God as if nothing were going on. The LORD reprimanded, "Have you not just now called to me, 'My father, you are the friend of my youth—will he be angry forever, will he be indignant to the end?' Behold, you have spoken, but you have done all the evil that you could" (Jer 3:4–5). The idea that God would stop being angry with sin by simply giving it time was dismissive of his holiness. There was no repentance, no turning away from idols or turning from evil. They simply assumed that time heals all wounds and God would get over it. The New Testament is no less opposed to idolatry and evil. It should not be a surprise to us if we continue to treat God as a mate, instead of the holy Creator and Judge of all, that he will not listen to our prayers.

Jeremiah Was Commanded Not Pray for Judah

On several occasions, Jeremiah was told by God to not pray for the people. He was commanded to go to the temple, and there demand that people change their ways, that is, act justly and stop following idols. If the people had listened and repented, then God would have relented and not brought judgement upon them. But they believed that they could have it both ways—steal, murder, commit adultery and lie, worship Baal and still come to the temple of God. The expectation was that the presence of the temple would keep away their enemies. Their trust was in the completely wrong place (Jer 7:1–15). Therefore, the LORD commanded Jeremiah:

"As for you, do not pray for this people, or lift up a cry or prayer for them, and do not intercede with me, for I will not hear you. Do you not see what they are doing in the cities of Judah and in the streets of Jerusalem? The children gather wood, the fathers kindle fire, and the women knead dough, to make cakes for the queen of heaven. And they pour out drink offerings to other gods, to provoke me to anger. Is it I whom they provoke? declares the LORD. Is it not themselves, to their own shame?" (Jer 7:16–19)

Everyone was involved in idolatry: men, women and children. No one was innocent. You have probably been taught to pray for the lost, for the wicked, as have I. Yet here Jeremiah was told that the LORD had made up his mind to judge the people and to not have mercy because of what they were doing. So, he was not to pray or ask for the judgement to stop because God would not hear. God would not hear because his patience had run out. This suggests that there is a point of no return and a time when God will not hear prayer for people who have known the truth and yet refused to listen to the truth and repent. It is sobering to think that there is only a finite number of opportunities before judgement falls.

Nonetheless, knowing what was coming against Judah and its people, Jeremiah prayed anyway.

"I know, O LORD, that the way of man is not in himself, that it is not in man who walks to direct his steps. Correct me, O LORD, but in justice; not in your anger, lest you bring me to nothing. Pour out your wrath on the nations that know you not, and on the peoples that call not on your name, for they have devoured Jacob; they have devoured him and consumed him, and have laid waste his habitation." (Jer 10:23–25)

Jeremiah knew that God is totally sovereign over what happens to people, even to directing the steps of people, and he prayed accordingly. Jeremiah asked for merciful correction for himself rather than all out punishment. Then, he prayed that God's judgement would be upon godless people from other nations who attacked God's people in Judah. The land of Judah was given by God according to his promise; they were his people, and he was their God (Exod 6:7; Lev 26:12). This was why Jeremiah could pray such a prayer, even though it seems to be contrary to what God told him not to do. There was no rebuke from the LORD for asking for this. Ultimately, this prayer was answered when God judged the Babylonians (Jer 12:14–17; 51:55–56), but that was many years into the future.

Again, Jeremiah was commanded to tell the people that they had broken the covenant with the LORD. There was a curse on anyone who does not obey the covenant that God set up. There was a promise of blessing for obedience. The people of Judah still hoped for the blessings of obedience when in reality they did not listen to God or obey him. Consequently, the covenant curses would come upon them. They had conspired together to return to the false gods of their ancestors (Jer 11:1–10). "Therefore, thus says the LORD, Behold, I am bringing disaster upon them that they cannot escape. Though they cry to me, I will not listen to them" (Jer 11:11). Prayer was useless in this situation. The LORD had determined to punish their sin and would not stop the coming judgement. Nor would prayer to worthless false gods be of any value because idols cannot help anyone (Jer 11:12). Consequently, God repeated his command to Jeremiah to not pray. "Therefore do not pray for this people, or lift up a cry or prayer on their behalf, for I will not listen when they call to me in the time of their trouble" (Jer 11:14).

A third time Jeremiah was told not to pray for the people of Judah. At this point a drought had come upon Judah, there was no water in the cisterns, no rain on the land, no grass in the fields and nothing for animals to eat (Jer 14:1–6). A prayer is recorded here in Jer 14.

> "Though our iniquities testify against us, act, O LORD, for your name's sake; for our backslidings are many; we have sinned against you. O you hope of Israel, its saviour in time of trouble, why should you be like a stranger in the land, like a traveller who turns aside to tarry for a night? Why should you be like a man confused, like a mighty warrior who cannot save? Yet you, O LORD, are in the midst of us, and we are called by your name; do not leave us." (Jer 14:7–9)

Opinions vary regarding this prayer. It seems incongruous for the people of Judah to suddenly confess their sins and agree that the famine was the result of those sins. Some explanation is in order. The form of the prayer is a lament. A lament usually includes a complaint of some kind, a confession of sin, an affirmation of confidence in God and a pledge of thanks when the prayer is answered. The order is different in this prayer, but the main elements are there. Some different options are possible here: either Jeremiah prayed for the people, or he demonstrated an appropriate kind of prayer for them to copy, or perhaps this was a corporate prayer. It was strange that the people suddenly admitted to their sin. But if they did so, the impression one gets from this prayer is that they were going through the motions in order to manipulate the LORD into taking away the drought, rather than showing the desire to return to him. Their expectation was that the LORD God should be present in Israel. This was his job. He existed to fix things for them.

The response of God to this prayer was to reiterate that the people of Judah loved to wander away from him, and he would punish them for their sinful rebellion against him (Jer 14:10). Then Jeremiah was told for the third time not to pray for the people. "The LORD said to me: 'Do not pray for the welfare of this people. Though they fast, I will not hear their cry, and though they offer burnt offering and grain offering, I will not accept them. But I will consume them by the sword, by famine, and by pestilence'" (Jer 14:11–12). Jeremiah prayed about this word from God because he was wondering whether the punishment was going to arrive when other prophets were saying the opposite. The LORD confirmed for Jeremiah that the prophets were prophesying lies. Therefore, an even worse punishment would come upon them than what would upon the rest of the people (Jer 14:13–16).

In response, there was another prayer to the LORD (see comments regarding who prayed the prayer above).

> "Have you utterly rejected Judah? Does your soul loathe Zion? Why have you struck us down so that there is no healing for us? We looked for peace, but no good came; for a time of healing, but behold, terror. We acknowledge our wickedness, O LORD, and the iniquity of our fathers, for we have sinned against you. Do not spurn us, for your name's sake; do not dishonour your glorious throne; remember and do not break your covenant with us. Are there any among the false gods of the nations that can bring rain? Or can the heavens give showers? Are you not he, O LORD our God? We set our hope on you, for you do all these things." (Jer 14:19–22)

This prayer was very similar to prayers that some in Kings prayed. At those other times, the LORD was merciful and brought deliverance. But this time, he was determined to punish the sin of the people. There was no genuine repentance. They did not want to turn back to their God.

That God was not going to answer this is made clear by the next verse. "Then the LORD said to me, 'Though Moses and Samuel stood before me, yet my heart would not turn toward this people. Send them out of my sight, and let them go!'" (Jer 15:1). More oracles of destruction follow this statement (Jer 15:3–9). This indicates that the form of the prayer is not what results in the answer we desire. God is not swayed by particular words in a particular order. He cannot be manipulated. His holiness is absolute; he cannot be other than himself. God is not fooled by our half-hearted repentance, because he sees the heart. Nor could the prophet repent on behalf of the people if they themselves continued in their sin.

Four times God told Jeremiah to stop praying for Judah. He would punish the people for their sin, no matter what. This is another reminder that calling out to the LORD for help when you have completely ignored him and will not listen to him is fruitless. He will not listen. It is also frequently fruitless praying for people to experience peace and safety when they are in rebellion against God. Often it is necessary for people to go through some form of suffering in order to turn them away from their sin. As long as sin seems to be a good thing and idols appear to be true gods, sinners are content to stay where they are. Why turn to God if everything is going the way you want it? But, for some, disaster can have the effect of waking people up to the uselessness of what they have been relying on, and open their hearts to the truth and their need for the true God.

Reflection Questions / Journal Prompts

1. Recall a time when you sensed the Holy Spirit saying that it was too late to pray for an individual or group. Did you continue to pray or not?
2. Reflect on the difference between praying the right words and having your heart right before God.

Part 2

Jeremiah Prayed about His Calling

ON THE OTHER HAND, Jeremiah prayed several times regarding himself and his calling. A large percentage of these prayers were complaints. This began when Jeremiah was called by God to be a prophet. "Now the word of the LORD came to me, saying, 'Before I formed you in the womb I knew you, and before you were born I consecrated you; I appointed you a prophet to the nations.' Then I said, 'Ah, Lord GOD! Behold, I do not know how to speak, for I am only a youth'" (Jer 1:4–6). Jeremiah's complaint about being called by God is reminiscent of what Moses did at the burning bush. Yet the LORD did not take No for an answer and told Jeremiah to go where he was sent and speak what he was told to say (Jer 1:7).

Jeremiah was not happy about being a prophet. He experienced a great deal of rejection and persecution because of his calling. He complained to God about this on more than one occasion. In the first instance, the LORD showed Jeremiah that people were plotting against him. He had been like a lamb to the slaughter because the people of Anathoth, Jeremiah's hometown, wanted to cut him down like a tree, to kill him so that no one would remember his name. This revelation prompted Jeremiah to pray that God would judge them and bring vengeance on them. And the LORD promised that he would punish them severely (Jer 11:18–23). This was the point at which Jeremiah began complaining to God.

> "Righteous are you, O LORD, when I complain to you; yet I would plead my case before you. Why does the way of the wicked prosper? Why do all who are treacherous thrive? You plant them, and they take root; they grow and produce fruit; you are near in their mouth and far from their heart. But

you, O LORD, know me; you see me, and test my heart toward you. Pull them out like sheep for the slaughter, and set them apart for the day of slaughter. How long will the land mourn and the grass of every field wither? For the evil of those who dwell in it the beasts and the birds are swept away, because they said, 'He will not see our latter end.'" (Jer 12:1–4)

Although Jeremiah had been faithfully speaking against the wicked, God's judgement against them had not yet arrived. Jeremiah's complaint was that the wicked were still doing well. These people were established and fruitful, even as they professed their love of God with their mouths and denied it with their lives. Jeremiah's prayer was similar to one the psalmist prayed (see e.g., Ps 73). Many of us have prayed prayers like this. It seems like all the talk of God judging the wicked is nothing but empty promises because they are all doing just fine. Being a Christian is hard work; it involves sacrifices of time and money. Even in the western world, Christians are frequently persona non grata. Yet evil people simply get away with whatever they please. What is God doing?

Jeremiah's prayer was that the wicked would be like sheep for the slaughter. We can confidently pray for the punishment of the wicked. The book of Revelation contains prayers like this (Rev 6:10). What we cannot do is make it happen. That is not up to us (Rom 12:19; Heb 10:30). Ours is to trust that God will judge justly and will not allow wickedness to go on unchecked forever. Trust in the justice of God and his sovereignty is vital because God's judgement may be delayed until the Day of Judgement itself.

A further prayer of complaint is found in Jer 15. First, Jeremiah uttered words that suggest he was seriously depressed. "Woe is me, my mother, that you bore me, a man of strife and contention to the whole land!

I have not lent, nor have I borrowed, yet all of them curse me" (Jer 15:10). It is a hard task to proclaim judgement upon your own people. No one appreciates the person who does this. Jeremiah was not a popular man, and he was tired of this to the point of wishing that he had never been born. No one chooses birth or the call of God. These are given to us, and we must accept what God has given. Trust in God includes trust in the call of God upon our lives, whether that call be to our liking or not.

Despite this despairing prayer, the LORD promised to deliver Jeremiah (Jer 15:11). But Jeremiah's complaint was not over.

> "O LORD, you know; remember me and visit me, and take vengeance for me on my persecutors. In your forbearance take me not away; know that for your sake I bear reproach. Your words were found, and I ate them, and your words became to me a joy and the delight of my heart, for I am called by your name, O LORD, God of hosts. I did not sit in the company of revellers, nor did I rejoice; I sat alone, because your hand was upon me, for you had filled me with indignation. Why is my pain unceasing, my wound incurable, refusing to be healed? Will you be to me like a deceitful brook, like waters that fail?" (Jer 15:15–18)

Jeremiah was obedient to the call of God upon his life. He took the words of God inside himself and loved God's word. He knew that he belonged to God. He kept himself from sin and from sinners. Yet, Jeremiah was in pain from the endless persecution, feeling like he was deserted by God. These seem like understandable feelings, but sometimes complaining to God is not the most helpful thing to do, as God's response to the complaint makes plain.

God's response to Jeremiah's complaint was surprising and encouraging at the same time. First of all, the LORD told Jeremiah to repent so that he could serve God (Jer 15:19). If Jeremiah loved God's word and kept himself from sin, what did he need to repent of? God is pleased by faith, but Jeremiah had lost faith in God to some extent at this point. The LORD had already promised that he would deliver Jeremiah for good purpose. Yet, Jeremiah plainly did not believe him, because he accused God of being deceitful and unhelpful. The LORD had determined to use Jeremiah as his prophet before he was even born (Jer 1:5). His choice was, therefore, not based on Jeremiah's particular actions. But faith is necessary in relationship with God and in his service. That faith can come from hearing the word of God, and in this case, it was necessary for Jeremiah's faith to hear the rebuke from God.

The remainder of God's response to Jeremiah's complaint was a promise to use Jeremiah if he spoke worthy not worthless words. He was told not to turn to the people, not to become like them in their sinful rejection of God. God's promise to Jeremiah was that he would become a bronze wall, and he would not be overcome because God would be with him and deliver him from the wicked people who wanted to harm him (Jer 15:19–21). God is faithful to his promises, but sometimes those promises are conditional. These particular promises were conditional on Jeremiah repenting and turning back to the God he had abandoned faith in.

It is possible that our complaints against God are actually hindering the answers to our prayers, not because they are complaints but because they represent a lack of trust in God. God does not have to answer us in the way we ask, in order to demonstrate who he is. Yet sometimes he does. He wants to use his people in his work in the world, as he wanted to use Jeremiah. His work cannot be thwarted by our lack of faith but our participation in that work may well be curtailed by that same lack of trust. Therefore, let us pray in trust that whatever happens in life is under the control of God and he is neither absent nor deceitful in what he says.

In the midst of complaints, Jeremiah's prayers were often full of praise. "O LORD, my strength and my stronghold, my refuge in the day of trouble, to you shall the nations come from the ends of the earth and say: 'Our fathers have inherited nothing but lies, worthless things in which there is no profit. Can man make for himself gods? Such are not gods!'" (Jer 16:19–20). Here he expressed confidence that the God of Israel is alone God. And God replied with an oracle of instruction about his might (Jer 16:21–17:11). This set Jeremiah off into another prayer of complaint about his persecutors.

> "O LORD, the hope of Israel, all who forsake you shall be put to shame; those who turn away from you shall be written in the earth, for they have forsaken the LORD, the fountain of living water. Heal me, O LORD, and I shall be healed; save me, and I shall be saved, for you are my praise. Behold, they say to me, 'Where is the word of the LORD? Let it come!' I have not run away from being your shepherd, nor have I desired the day of sickness. You know what came out of my lips; it was before your face. Be not a terror to me; you are my refuge in the day of disaster. Let those be put to shame who persecute me, but let me not be put to shame; let them be dismayed, but let me not be dismayed; bring upon them the day of disaster; destroy them with double destruction!" (Jer 17:13–18)

Jeremiah's plea came from one who was obedient to God when all around him stood against him. Jeremiah longed for the persecution to stop. He wanted God to terrorise those who persecuted him. There is no response from God recorded in this chapter. The poetry in Jer 17 gives way to prose, and there God told Jeremiah to go and prophesy against the people. There was no reassurance of God's protection against enemies, no comfort that God was with him. This has been the experience in my own life, that there are only so many times God will offer comfort and assurance. Beyond that, we must exercise faith in what God has already spoken. This is part of being a mature believer. God should have no need to continually bolster up those who have walked with him for years. Pray and trust that God has heard and that his promises are true.

There is yet another prayer in Jer 18, after Jeremiah prophesied at the potter's house and the people plotted against Jeremiah. In it, Jeremiah asked that his accusers would be punished—their children given over to starvation and their wives become childless widows. He asked that God would not forget their plots against him (Jer 18:1–23). Again, there was no response from the LORD to this plea, except a command to prophesy further (Jer 19:1–13). It seems that neither rebuke nor promise was needed here. God had already spoken to Jeremiah about this very thing many times, but Jeremiah felt the need to get his concerns, anxiety and anger off his chest.

After this, Jeremiah was arrested and put in the stocks for a day. Jeremiah then prophesied against his captor (Jer 20:1–6). The experience was too much for Jeremiah and he again complained to God.

> "O LORD, you have deceived me, and I was deceived; you are stronger than I, and you have prevailed. I have become a laughingstock all the day; everyone mocks me. For whenever I speak, I cry out, I shout, 'Violence and destruction!' For the word of the LORD has become for me a reproach and derision all day long. If I say, 'I will not mention him, or speak any more in his name,' there is in my

heart as it were a burning fire shut up in my bones, and I am weary with holding it in, and I cannot." (Jer 20:7–9)

For Jeremiah, being a prophet was a no-win situation and he told God exactly that. He felt like God had deceived him and made him the butt of every person's jokes. Telling the truth was repaid with persecution. But the opposite action by Jeremiah, that is, keeping quiet, did not help him because it was like a fire inside him that he could not hold in. Speaking or not speaking, Jeremiah was unhappy.

Yet there was good news in that Jeremiah expressed some faith. Even though everyone was out to get him, even his friends, the LORD was with him. He had confidence that God would fight on his side against those who persecuted him (Jer 20:10–11). This confidence in God was more than Jeremiah had had for some time. He had complained repeatedly and did not seem to hold tight to God's words to him, despite prophesying God's words to the people. He expressed his confidence in praise. "O LORD of hosts, who tests the righteous, who sees the heart and the mind, let me see your vengeance upon them, for to you have I committed my cause. Sing to the LORD; praise the LORD! For he has delivered the life of the needy from the hand of evildoers" (Jer 20:12–13).

But then the unstable nature of Jeremiah's depression was evident once more. He cursed the day he was born and wished that no one had ever announced his birth. Jeremiah regretted that his mother's womb was not his tomb because life outside the womb was full of sorrow and shame (Jer 20:14–18). One minute he was up praying and praising God for his deliverance and the next he was wishing that he were never born.

This prophet prayed such a range of emotions that he provides an example to those who struggle with volatile emotional states. I don't want to say that trust in God is optional, because it is not. Even in the midst of a crisis and deep depression, there is need for such trust. But the fact that we have such a rollercoaster of prayer recorded is testimony to the fact that God's holy people, even those who heard directly from God himself, are sometimes subject to great changes of emotions. There is no point in pretence in prayer, as if God did not know our hearts and our thoughts. He was well aware of Jeremiah's pain. He was also aware that in the midst of his pain, Jeremiah set his mind to praise God, even though he slipped even further down afterwards. This is a realistic view of prayer. It is not true that prayer will always lift your mood or solve your emotional pain. But that does not mean we cannot bring these things to God.

Reflection Questions / Journal Prompts

1. If you are aware of God's call upon your life, do you complain about this to God? How has he responded to you?
2. When your mental health is unstable, take your concerns to the LORD in prayer, trusting that he knows and understands what you are experiencing.

Part 3

Bad and Good Prayer Requests

AS THE BOOK OF JEREMIAH progresses, the situation with the Babylonians was clearly getting worse. Jeremiah received some requests to inquire of God. The first was from the king. King Zedekiah sent some priests to Jeremiah and asked, "Inquire of the LORD for us, for Nebuchadnezzar king of Babylon is making war against us. Perhaps the LORD will deal with us according to all his wonderful deeds and will make him withdraw from us'" (Jer 21:2). On the surface this request might suggest some piety on behalf of the king. After all, he referred to God's wonderful deeds in the past as did several good kings previously, and they received miraculous deliverance. However, 2 Kgs 24:19 calls Zedekiah a king who "did what was evil in the sight of the LORD." Hence his inquiry from God was not so much from faith as desperation, as if God is the miracle genie. The king must have heard Jeremiah's calls to repentance and yet in this request he did not acknowledge his sin.

This kind of prayer request might sometimes fool us into believing that the person making the request has grasped the greatness of God and is even on the verge of faith. Sometimes that is the case. But sometimes, as with king Zedekiah, it is just a matter of a you've-got-to-be-in-it-to-win-it sort of attitude. Perhaps God will solve their problem, but if not, they will try the next thing and the next. There is no real faith there. They are simply willing to use God for their own ends. Jeremiah's reply to the king is instructive. He repeated his prophecies of destruction against Judah and Jerusalem and included something against the king himself (Jer 21:3–14). Jeremiah did not indulge the king by praying to the LORD for him. He already knew the answer, and the king should have known it also, but he did not want to know. Rather than seeking God to fix unbelievers' problems, we would perhaps do better to point them to God's written word. Wisdom is called for here.

Jerusalem fell to the Babylonians. The situation after this was difficult for those who were not killed or carted away into exile. The people left in the land were afraid and wanted to flee to Egypt (Jer 41:16–17). They went to Jeremiah and asked him to pray and ask God what to do, and Jeremiah agreed. The people swore that they would obey God whatever the answer was, either good or bad (Jer 42:1–6). Ten days later, Jeremiah heard from the LORD, who commanded the people to stay in the land because he would deliver them from the king of Babylon. He told them that if they insisted on going to Egypt then they would all die by sword, famine or plague. The LORD would be angry with their disobedience (Jer 42:7–18).

Jeremiah rebuked the people,

> "The LORD has said to you, O remnant of Judah, 'Do not
> go to Egypt.' Know for a certainty that I have warned you
> this day that you have gone astray at the cost of your lives.
> For you sent me to the LORD your God, saying, 'Pray for us
> to the LORD our God, and whatever the LORD our God
> says declare to us and we will do it.' And I have this day
> declared it to you, but you have not obeyed the voice of the
> LORD your God in anything that he sent me to tell you."
> (Jer 42:19–21)

The people became angry with Jeremiah and accused him of being a
liar. So, the people, still afraid of the Babylonians, disobeyed God's
command through the prophet and went to Egypt, dragging Jeremiah
with them (Jer 43:1–7).

It is a dangerous thing to pray when you have already decided what
you are going to do. We often want God to simply endorse our choices
instead of asking with the genuine intention of obeying what God says.
Just because someone piously asks for prayer about a decision, this does
not always mean that the person wants to know what God says. This is
still true today. The Bible gives us a great deal of plain instruction about
how to live. But there are times when we go to prayer with the hope
that we will receive a different message, a more palatable message about
our lives. This is no different to what the survivors of Judah did when
they asked Jeremiah to pray.

Nonetheless, there was hope for those who accepted God's judgement
upon their sin. Although Hananiah prophesied falsely that the exile
would last only two years (Jer 28:1–4), Jeremiah declared correctly
that it would be seventy years long (Jer 25:11–12; 29:10). He wrote
a letter to the exiles that they must settle down in Babylon, instead

of expecting to come home soon. He instructed them, "But seek the welfare of the city where I have sent you into exile, and pray to the LORD on its behalf, for in its welfare you will find your welfare" (Jer 29:7). Prayer for the welfare of the Babylonians, who had just come and destroyed Judah and enslaved her people, must have been a difficult thing to do. Yet, God's plans for his people are no short-term fix. He would transform the people in their time in exile. Part of that was accepting that this situation was from God and, therefore, they must seek to live as godly, praying people in the place where they lived.

Christians, also, must choose to not have an escapist mentality. We are "sojourners and exiles" (1 Pet 2:11) in this world until the Lord Jesus returns. But we cannot simply hold on until then, ignoring what is happening in the place in which we have been given by God to live (see Acts 17:26). Praying for the people among whom we live is a Christian occupation and vocation. The real work of God does not begin later, in heaven, but now in the world in which we are placed for the duration of our exile from our heavenly home.

Signs of Future Hope

Like Isaiah, Jeremiah offered a vision of restoration and transformation for Israel (Jer 29:10–14). Among these great promises regarding the end of exile was a promise that the people would pray to the LORD, and he would hear them. "Then you will call upon me and come and pray to me, and I will hear you" (Jer 29:12). In this context, praying to God and being heard by him are tied up with return to the land, the place of God's presence and favour. Given that God had refused to listen to the people throughout Jeremiah, and even refused to allow Jeremiah to pray for them, the promise was a powerful one. The exile was a time of chastisement and an opportunity to be restored to their God. Those who returned would be different. Yet the return from exile proved far less glorious than anyone expected and the transformation somewhat disappointing, pointing forward to a later time in the future, when the coming of Christ would transform the world and the Holy Spirit would totally transform people so that they would cast aside their idols, and pray to the true God and he would hear them.

Another sign of hope for the future came in the form of the LORD commanding Jeremiah to buy a field. At that point, Jeremiah was confined to the courtyard of the palace and the Babylonians were making siege against Jerusalem. Then God told Jeremiah to buy a piece of land belonging to his relative, which he did, putting the deed of purchase in a clay jar in order to keep it for a long time (Jer 32:1–15). Then Jeremiah prayed (Jer 32:16).

> "Ah, Lord GOD! It is you who have made the heavens and the earth by your great power and by your outstretched arm! Nothing is too hard for you. You show steadfast love to thousands, but you repay the guilt of fathers to their children after them, O great and mighty God, whose name is the LORD of hosts, great in counsel and mighty in deed, whose eyes are open to all the ways of the children of man, rewarding each one according to his ways and according to the fruit of his deeds. You have shown signs and wonders in the land of Egypt, and to this day in Israel and among all mankind, and have made a name for yourself, as at this day. You brought your people Israel out of the land of Egypt with signs and wonders, with a strong hand and outstretched arm, and with great terror. And you gave them this land, which you swore to their fathers to give them, a land flowing with milk and honey. And they entered and took possession of it. But they did not obey your voice or walk in your law. They did nothing of all you commanded them to do. Therefore you have made all this disaster come upon them." (Jer 32:17–23)

This prayer is a surprising one in a sense, because out of eight verses, six are about God's redemptive work in the history of Israel. Jeremiah began his prayer with praise for God as Creator and a reiteration of God's greatness. He emphasised the fact that the LORD is Judge of people and punishes sins. He recapped the truth that God brought Israel out of Egypt and gave them the land. But the people did not obey God and consequently, the LORD brought disaster upon them. Only when Jeremiah had given a biblical context, did he turn to his present situation and ask his question of the LORD.

> "Behold, the siege mounds have come up to the city to take it, and because of sword and famine and pestilence the city is given into the hands of the Chaldeans who are fighting against it. What you spoke has come to pass, and behold, you see it. Yet you, O Lord GOD, have said to me, 'Buy the field for money and get witnesses'—though the city is given into the hands of the Chaldeans.'" (Jer 32:24–25)

The situation was obviously dire, and Jeremiah's indirect question suggested that although he had obeyed the instruction to buy the land, he was wondering why he was doing so. Perhaps the long introduction before Jeremiah got to his point was by way of saying that he trusted in God's power and might, and agreed with the punishment that was coming upon them. But he wanted to know the purpose of the land deed if the end was nigh. God's answer to Jeremiah was to reiterate that he would punish the heinous sin of the people of Judah by sending the Babylonians. Yet restoration would come. God promised to bring people back to the land, to transform them, make an everlasting covenant with them, and bless them. All this explained why Jeremiah was told to buy land; one day land would again be bought and sold in Judah (Jer 32:26–44).

In regard to prayer, Jeremiah set an example for Christians now. He did not understand why he was doing what God commanded, but he did it anyway. Only then did he set to pray about it. Even then, Jeremiah spent time in his prayer considering who God is and what he had done in the past. His focus was on both the great deeds of the LORD and the sinfulness of the people. All these things made sense of the present situation for him. Not until the end did Jeremiah obliquely ask why. Unlike his earlier prayers, there was far more faith for us to emulate here. We do not always need to know in advance why. But we can ask; God is able to provide an answer to the why question. In this case there was an answer, but sometimes there is not. There are questions God does not seem to answer. In those we must trust him. But seeking for God to reveal things to us is not wrong or foolish. The great difference between Jeremiah and Christians now is that we should not seek for direct revelation but expect God to open his word to us so that we can understand what he is doing and how his actions and commands provide us with hope for the future.

Reflection Questions / Journal Prompts

1. Recall situations in which you prayed as if God is the miracle genie, and compare these to a time when you prayed with true respect, knowing that God is above all.
2. Compose a prayer that recounts the wonderous deeds of God in the past. Thank him for the hope of a future with him.

Conclusion

The book of Jeremiah is full of prayer. Even though people apart from the prophet prayed, the LORD did not bless those prayers. He was not pleased with the idolatry of the people, nor was he pleased with their fake piety. He knows what is in the hearts of humans, that we are out to get what we want from God rather than desiring true relationship and obedience. God judged the people of Judah and their worthless prayers. Such a judgement is a reason to take stock of our lives and our prayer lives. Since it is difficult to see our own sin and repent of it, ask God to show you your sin and grant you the gift of repentance (see Acts 5:31) in order that you might gain a better relationship with him.

Many times, God told Jeremiah to stop praying for the people of Judah because God would not relent from punishing them. Jeremiah sometimes prayed for mercy anyway. Although we want to stop people's pain, sometimes difficulties are the only means which will get people to think about their need of God. Therefore, praying for our unsaved friends and family that nothing bad will happen to them may not be the best strategy. Pray instead that God's judgement—whether it is giving them over to their sin (Rom 1:24–28) or natural disasters or war—will bring repentance and revival.

Jeremiah also complained a great deal about his calling as a prophet. He suffered for this calling and wished it would go away. His mental health went up and down like the waves of the sea. His prayers to God in the midst of his pain are an indication that, for those of us who have unstable mental health, we may bring our fluctuating emotions to God in prayer. But do so in faith rather than in anger or despair, because God uses people with faith to accomplish his purposes in the world. We may trust God in the midst of difficulties and even in depression and pray accordingly.

Despite the inevitability of judgement, there was hope in the book. There would be a future restoration of relationship between Judah and their God. Christ is our hope (1 Cor 1:27; 1 Thess 1:3; Titus 2:13). He restores relationship with God for humanity. Yet we know that there is more to come. For this we pray, "Come Lord Jesus" (Rev 22:20).

Daniel: Prayer for a Lifetime

D aniel was carried off into exile in Babylon by Nebuchadnezzar as a young man. He was chosen to be trained to serve the king of Babylon because of his noble heritage, his pleasing appearance and intelligence (Dan 1:3–4). Daniel lived in Babylon a long time and survived through the reigns of several kings. Because of Daniel's prayers, God equipped Daniel to interpret dreams and thus serve the king. His prayer life was more important to him than being trouble-free. Daniel knew the word of God and used this as the basis for how he prayed. His piety remained strong throughout his lifetime.

Daniel Was Different

When Daniel was first chosen for the service of the king, he was given an allotted amount of food and wine from the king's table. Daniel resolved not to eat the king's food because he did not want to be defiled by it (Dan 1:5, 8). The guards did not want to allow Daniel and his Jewish companions to eat only vegetables because they thought he would get weak, and they would get into trouble. But God blessed Daniel's choice and made them healthier than anyone else (Dan 1:9–16).

It is notable in our study of prayer that Daniel did not pray about this decision. It is possible that the prayer was not recorded, but it is equally possible that Daniel based his decision purely on the law of Moses, which forbids certain foods for the people of Israel (Lev 11). He did not need to pray about whether to eat foods that were likely to be unlawful for him. He simply acted in faith in order to guarantee his obedience to Jewish dietary restrictions, because obeying God was foremost in his mind. It is actually foolish to pray about something

God has already commanded very clearly in his word. Why would we do so? Perhaps because we would prefer God to say something different.

Daniel and his companions were considered wiser and more understanding than all the magicians and enchanters in the kingdom (Dan 1:20). This was good, but it also resulted in Daniel being lumped together with the astrologers. When the king had a disturbing dream, he asked his magicians to interpret the dream. They wanted to know what the dream was, but the king made things impossible by asking them to tell him the dream as well as interpret it. None of them could do this, because, as they correctly observed, only the gods can reveal such things. The king was very angry and decreed that all the wise men be executed. At this point, Daniel and his companions were rounded up to be executed also. But Daniel asked for time to interpret the dream (Dan 2:1–16).

"Then Daniel went to his house and made the matter known to Hananiah, Mishael, and Azariah, his companions, and told them to seek mercy from the God of heaven concerning this mystery, so that Daniel and his companions might not be destroyed with the rest of the wise men of Babylon" (Dan 2:17–18). The situation they were caught up in was bleak. Yet Daniel and his Israelite companions had done nothing wrong. By the same token, Daniel knew as well as the astrologers that he could not know and interpret the king's dream on his own without some revelation from God. Asking for time to interpret the dream implied a belief that God could, maybe even would, give Daniel an interpretation. Daniel did not just hope for the best but prayed together with the other Jews. They made no demand upon God, but instead sought mercy from God. Being in exile, each was well aware of the absolute sovereignty and holiness of God.

Then the mystery was revealed to Daniel in a vision of the night. Then Daniel blessed the God of heaven. Daniel answered and said: "Blessed be the name of God forever and ever, to whom belong wisdom and might. He changes times and seasons; he removes kings and sets up kings; he gives wisdom to the wise and knowledge to those who have understanding; he reveals deep and hidden things; he knows what is in the darkness, and the light dwells with him. To you, O God of my fathers, I give thanks and praise, for you have given me wisdom and might, and have now made known to me what we asked of you, for you have made known to us the king's matter." (Dan 2:19–23)

Their prayer for mercy was answered swiftly. Daniel's immediate response was praise to God. His praise revolved around the wonder of God's sovereignty over knowledge, seasons and kings, and over what is hidden in darkness. Daniel specifically called God "God of my fathers" to distinguish the Jewish God from the false gods of Babylon, who clearly did not reveal mysteries. Daniel was stuck in Babylon, surrounded by people who worshipped false gods, and subject to a king who could at whim decide to execute him, but he was confident that the God of Israel was sovereign over all aspects of this situation. When Daniel received the revelation, he did not take credit for himself but told that king that it was God who revealed the dream and interpretation (Dan 2:27–28). Daniel gave glory to God both before and after his prayer was answered.

The lesson here is that instead of concentrating on whatever intractable situation we find ourselves in, it is always best to go to God and seek his mercy. "Let us then with confidence draw near to the throne of grace, that we may receive mercy and find grace to help in time of need" (Heb 4:16). Not every aspect of Daniel's situation changed because of his prayer; he was still a slave in a foreign land at the end of the day. Not every aspect of our situation will necessarily change when we pray. But we can be confident that the sovereignty of God has not been diminished with time. Therefore, let us not forget to thank him for who he is and what he has done, both in the past and in providing mercy and help in the present.

Prayer and Death

Many years went by—Nebuchadnezzar died, and his grandson Belshazzar was conquered by the Medes and Persians—before we are told anything further about Daniel's prayer life. Daniel was appointed as a satrap, an official in Babylon, and he did his job well, even better than all the other officials in the kingdom. Consequently, the other officials became jealous and conspired together to find a way to do away with Daniel. Since he was not corrupt in any way, they decided that the only way to get him in trouble would have to be in relation to the law of his God. So the officials advised the king to make a law stating that no one could pray to any god or human being, except the king, for thirty days. The punishment was to be thrown into the lion's den. The king agreed (Dan 6:1–9).

"When Daniel knew that the document had been signed, he went to his house where he had windows in his upper chamber open toward Jerusalem. He got down on his knees three times a day and prayed and gave thanks before his God, as he had done previously" (Dan 6:10). From this verse we learn several things. First of all, Daniel was in the habit of praying three times a day. He was in a foreign land, but he still sought out the God of Israel because he was a great man of faith (see Ezek 14:14). It is not stated explicitly, but it is likely that Daniel's constant prayer was the basis for his godly life and his ability to interpret dreams.

Secondly, Daniel prayed in the direction of Jerusalem, where the temple once stood (although it had been razed to the ground by the

Babylonians when they invaded Judah—2 Kgs 25:8–9; Jer 52:12–13; 2 Chr 36:19). He knew that the promise to Solomon that God would hear his people who prayed from exile (1 Kgs 8:46–49; 9:3) still stood.

Thirdly, and this is extremely significant, Daniel knew full well that praying like this was against the law of the king, under which he was enslaved. He did not stop praying just because the law of Persia and Media forbade this practice. The law of God was above the law of the land in which he lived; he was more concerned with pleasing God than with making his life easy. Not only this, but Daniel could have prayed from hiding but he did it in full view of his enemies. His confidence in God was such, that like Shadrach, Meshach and Abednego—who were thrown into the fiery furnace for not worshipping a giant statue of king Nebuchadnezzar (Dan 3)—Daniel was willing to die, but not willing to be disobedient. He trusted in his God and saw no reason to hide his trust in God.

Lastly, when a problem arose for Daniel, the first thing he did was pray, instead of protesting the injustice of it. Daniel's prayer habit was vindicated because, although he was thrown to the lions, God protected him from death (Dan 6:22).

The example of Daniel in prayer is helpful to us. As Christians, we are like exiles in a foreign land (1 Pet 1:1; 2:11). There will continually be issues with the godless cultures in which we live. Laws made by unbelieving governments will often be not to our liking or, more significantly, absolutely contrary to God's law. I shall not debate the value of protesting and petitioning governments to change laws, but I will say that prayer should be our first and our continual response to what happens in our country. We are fighting a battle that is not against flesh and blood, but against spiritual powers of wickedness (Eph 6:12). Do not give up. If Daniel could pray openly in the midst of Babylon, then we can pray privately (at least) in Australia.

Prayer Based on God's Promise to Jeremiah

Daniel had been in Babylon for many decades. He had served several kings, seen many visions, and held on to his integrity. We already know that Daniel was a man with a regular prayer life. But in Dan 9, we are given some insight into *how* Daniel prayed.

> In the first year of Darius the son of Ahasuerus, by descent a Mede, who was made king over the realm of the Chaldeans—in the first year of his reign, I, Daniel, perceived in the books the number of years that, according to the word of the LORD to Jeremiah the prophet, must pass before the end of the desolations of Jerusalem, namely, seventy years. Then I turned my face to the Lord God, seeking him by prayer and pleas for mercy with fasting and sackcloth and ashes. (Dan 9:1–3)

What drove Daniel to prayer was his reading of the Scripture, specifically the prophecy of the prophet Jeremiah regarding the end of the exile. He did not passively wait for the promised return to Judah. Daniel prayed. We often neglect what God has said, his great and precious promises (2 Pet 1:4) when we pray. If the godly people of Scripture prayed on the basis of God's word, then we too should pray according to God's word. We should not assume that just because God said something, that we have no need to pray about that. Epaphras was a New Testament example of this, who wrestled in prayer that the church would stand mature and complete in the will of God (Col 4:12). Assuredly, God desires these things, but our task is to join God in agreement through prayer that his will and word will come to pass. This is why we pray, "Your kingdom come" (Matt 6:10; Luke 11:2) in the Lord's Prayer. God desires it but we have been given a part to play in prayer so that the kingdom of God comes.

Daniel's prayer is described as "pleas for mercy". He did so with fasting, sackcloth and ashes, symbols of mourning and humility before God. The content of his prayer makes clear why this was so, beginning with "I prayed to the LORD my God and made confession" (Dan 9:4a). The thrust of this long prayer was the sin of Judah and a plea for mercy and forgiveness.

Daniel began with praise. "O Lord, the great and awesome God, who keeps covenant and steadfast love with those who love him and keep his commandments" (Dan 9:4b). The promises and the character of God were in the forefront. This was the ground on which Daniel prayed. The God of Israel is a covenant-keeping God. However, the promises of God are for those who love God and are obedient to him.

Daniel's prayer went on to confession on behalf of the people of Judah. "[W]e have sinned and done wrong and acted wickedly and rebelled, turning aside from your commandments and rules. We have not listened to your servants the prophets, who spoke in your name to our kings, our princes, and our fathers, and to all the people of the land" (Dan 9:5–6). Daniel himself was a righteous man, as attested by God (Ezek 14:14, 20), but he did not exclude himself from this list of wrongs.

Again, Daniel contrasted the righteousness of God and the shame of the people of Judah and Israel, who had been exiled from the land because of their sin against God. Shame was theirs because everyone—including kings and princes—had sinned. God is merciful and forgiving, which the people desperately needed because they were rebellious and disobedient, having failed to obey God's laws. This was true of the whole nation—both Judah and Israel. Rightfully, according to the curses of that Law of Moses, God had punished them because of their sin (Dan 9:7–11). Twice Daniel contrasted the nature of God with the nature of God's people. He did not make Judah and Israel out to be deserving of an answer to prayer. Daniel's hope in this prayer was based in God's character, not in himself, and most especially not in the righteousness of the people of Judah.

Daniel continued.

> "He has confirmed his words, which he spoke against us and against our rulers who ruled us, by bringing upon us a great calamity. For under the whole heaven there has not been done anything like what has been done against Jerusalem. As it is written in the Law of Moses, all this calamity has come upon us; yet we have not entreated the favour of the LORD our God, turning from our iniquities and gaining insight by your truth. Therefore the LORD has kept ready the calamity and has brought it upon us, for the LORD our God is righteous in all the works that he has done, and we have not obeyed his voice." (Dan 9:12–14)

This statement repeated the same theme, that God is righteous and the people of Judah and Israel were not. The exile was a devastating event, first the nation of Israel was carted off to Assyria (2 Kgs 17), and then just over a hundred years later, having learned nothing from what happened to Israel, Judah was exiled to Babylon (2 Kgs 25). The shame of being cast out of the Promised Land was great and every nation around understood that Israel and Judah had been shamed (Deut 28:37; 2 Chr 29:8). Daniel confessed that despite the shame, the people had not sought God and turned from their sin. He repeated the truth that God is righteous in having inflicted this shame upon the people of Judah.

Then Daniel turned to petition.

> "And now, O Lord our God, who brought your people out of the land of Egypt with a mighty hand, and have made

a name for yourself, as at this day, we have sinned, we have done wickedly. O Lord, according to all your righteous acts, let your anger and your wrath turn away from your city Jerusalem, your holy hill, because for our sins, and for the iniquities of our fathers, Jerusalem and your people have become a byword among all who are around us." (Dan 9:15–16)

This petition focused on the past redeeming actions of God, that he rescued Israel from Egypt and thereby made a name for himself. God is great and truly deserves the obedience of his people and yet they sinned. Daniel pleaded for forgiveness for the people on the basis of God's righteous acts. Although the people had sinned grievously, they were still the people God chose, and Jerusalem was still the city in which God chose to have a temple built. The fact that God's people were experiencing the shame of exile and that Jerusalem lay in ruins may have an effect on God, whose name was associated with his people and that city.

"Now therefore, O our God, listen to the prayer of your servant and to his pleas for mercy, and for your own sake, O Lord, make your face to shine upon your sanctuary, which is desolate. O my God, incline your ear and hear. Open your eyes and see our desolations, and the city that is called by your name. For we do not present our pleas before you because of our righteousness, but because of your great mercy. O Lord, hear; O Lord, forgive. O Lord, pay attention and act. Delay not, for your own sake, O my God, because your city and your people are called by your name." (Dan 9:17–19)

In the last section of the prayer, Daniel pleaded for restoration to the land for the LORD's sake. Both the people and the city of Jerusalem were called by his name. The people were not righteous, and therefore human righteousness was no basis for prayer. However, God is merciful and therefore Daniel could ask in confidence. The only basis for Daniel's prayer was the word of God and the character of God.

It is foolish to try to persuade God to grant your prayer request based on something you have done. Even as godly people, do we have the right to expect God to give us anything at all? Yet, because of his own righteousness and faithfulness, because he made promises to his people, and because of God's mercy, he grants us answers to prayer. Not every prayer is answered with a Yes, but that is not my point here. When God gives answered prayer it is because of who he is rather than because of anything we have done.

We might ask how a righteous man can confess sin on behalf of others. Certainly, Daniel was a righteous man, but there is one more righteous than he, namely, the Lord Jesus. The very fact that we are forgiven is because Jesus confessed our sin to God. In dying upon the cross, he offered himself as a sin offering (Rom 8:3) on our behalf. It could not have been on his behalf since he had no sin of his own (2 Cor 5:21; 1 Pet 2:22; Heb 4:15). As God in the flesh, Jesus understands the nature of our sin far more than we ever can. His death upon the cross was a genuine acknowledgement of the sinfulness of humanity in all its depravity and rebellion against God. The horror of the cross reflects the horror of the depths of sin to which we have all stooped.

As believers, we can confess the sins of our nation and the church as we pray that God will move to transform both nation and church. This does not, however, imply that no one need confess their individual sins to God. What Daniel's prayer does not tell us is that only a few people went home from exile; many did not want to return home. For them there was no repentance. The prayers of Ezra and Nehemiah (in a later chapter) also show us that repentance on behalf of others only goes so far. Sin was still present in the exiles because their hearts had not been changed sufficiently by seventy years of captivity in a foreign land. Only Christ and his Spirit can truly change the heart.

Yes, it is good to confess that both nation and church have sinned, and to plead for forgiveness. And God will hear this type of prayer and move. But what can we expect God to do? Forgiveness is the fruit of a relationship with God, based on faith in the gospel. For unbelievers, there must be a turning to God in the gospel before they can be forgiven. Thus a prayer for forgiveness for our nation might be answered by having more people come to faith in Christ, not by direct, Christless forgiveness. The church is commanded at times to repent (Rev 2:5, 16; 21, 22; 3:3, 19). This entails each person within the church being brought to repentance as well as the body of Christ repenting together. If we acknowledged the sin of the church and asked God to forgive, then the Holy Spirit will work to reveal our sin and urge us to turn away from those sins. A prayer like Daniel's prayer about the sin of the nation does not imply that individuals do not need to repent of their own sins.

Conclusion

Daniel lived in Babylon most of his life. He was an example to Christians because he maintained his love for God and his word throughout his long life in exile. Daniel was a man of prayer. He prayed in times of trouble and refused to forsake times of prayer, even under threat of death. Daniel's longest recorded prayer was one of repentance on behalf of the nation. Throughout his life, Daniel based his decisions and his prayers on God's word, recorded in the Scriptures. He never stopped trusting that God's word is true. Daniel was a humble man, not expecting answers to prayer based upon his piety but instead based upon the character of God and God's past redemptive actions. We could do well to have a prayer life which remains consistent, humble and steeped in the word of God throughout our entire lives.

Reflection Questions / Journal Prompts

1. Recount a time when you trusted God to get you out of an impossible situation.
2. Consider how your prayer life has changed over time. Are the changes for the better or does it wax and wane as situations change for better or worse?
3. Think about steps you can take to have a more consistent and regular prayer life.
4. In what ways might your prayer life be improved by incorporating the word of God into your prayers?

Post-Exilic Prayers: Ezra and Nehemiah

So far, the book has examined prayers prior to the exile—prayers of the patriarchs, during the exodus, in the wilderness, during the time of judges, prayers of women, prayers of prophets and kings, plus prayers of some major written prophets. The prayers of Daniel and Esther took place during the exile. This chapter will consider some prayers prayed after the exile. After seventy years some people from the southern kingdom returned to the land of Judah—and became known as Jews. Ezra and Nehemiah were leaders in the post-exilic nation of Judah. Because of the exile, these leaders became more conscious of sin. Sin had been the cause of the exile and they did not want to repeat the suffering that went with being forced to live in a foreign land. This coloured the way people prayed after the exile.

Ezra

When Ezra, and the families returning from Babylon to Jerusalem with him, were camped before setting off, he prayed for safety.

> Then I proclaimed a fast there, at the river Ahava, that we might humble ourselves before our God, to seek from him a safe journey for ourselves, our children, and all our goods. For I was ashamed to ask the king for a band of soldiers and horsemen to protect us against the enemy on our way, since we had told the king, "The hand of our God is for good on all who seek him, and the power of his wrath is against all who forsake him." So we fasted and implored our God for this, and he listened to our entreaty. (Ezra 8:21–23)

There are two reasons given for this fasting and prayer. The first was so that the group would have a safe journey. A mixed group of men, women and children would have been vulnerable to raids from many different and hostile groups along the way. The group was not large compared to the potential dangers they faced. They carried valuables for the temple, which would have made attack by bandits likely. This was a good reason to ask for the LORD's protection. And indeed, the LORD answered their prayer and brought them all safely to Jerusalem (Ezra 8:31–32).

The second reason for the prayer was to demonstrate that the LORD is truly God. Since the group of Jews setting out for Jerusalem had told the king of Persia (the ruler of Babylon) that God was on their side, they could not then ask for soldiers to protect them on their journey. If they were not safe on the journey, it would look like their God was against them. Both the reputation of God and the people returning to Jerusalem were on the line. God is concerned to uphold his own glory. The people were concerned to demonstrate their faith in the true God. Thus, the people did not take this prayer lightly. They both prayed and fasted. Confidence in God is part of Christian witness to the world. By this, unbelievers can see that God's word is true, when we live by it. We can rely upon what God has promised in his word. But it is not wise to boast beyond this.

Ezra's second prayer was a prayer of repentance. After the people had returned and set up the temple, a problem arose. Some of the men of Judah, including some leaders, had married women from the nations around them. Ezra was so upset by this turn of events that he tore his clothes and sat down in grief. He was surrounded by others who were afraid of the consequences as set out in the word of God. At the time of the evening sacrifice, Ezra got up and prayed upon his knees (Ezra 9:1–5). His prayer of repentance was lengthy.

It began with shame. Ezra acknowledged that the sins of the people were so dreadful that their guilt rose to heaven. This was not new but had been going on since the beginning. The result had been that the Jews were subject to wars, exile and loss (Ezra 9:6–7). If we have no concept of the severity of sin, both our own and that of the wider people of God (not merely the world), then it is impossible to pray genuine prayers of repentance. Here, Ezra had grasped the horror of sin, how it ruins our relationship with God, and the deserved punishment that goes with it.

His prayer continued with praise for God's grace in allowing some to return from exile. Things were far from perfect since they were still slaves, subject to the king of Persia, but God had granted them freedom to repair the temple and the walls of Jerusalem (Ezra 9:8–9). Having experienced exile in Babylon, being forced to live far from home, and having seen the temple in ruins, Ezra understood what a privilege it was to be back on home soil and to be able to worship God in the sanctuary again. His praise was for God's faithfulness, that God had not abandoned his people to the consequences of their sin. Yet the grace of God had been abused, as we will see. It is difficult to appreciate the grace of God if we do not first appreciate the heinous nature of our sin.

> "And now, O our God, what shall we say after this? For we have forsaken your commandments, which you commanded by your servants the prophets, saying, 'The land that you are entering, to take possession of it, is a land impure with the impurity of the peoples of the lands, with their abominations that have filled it from end to end with their uncleanness. Therefore do not give your daughters to their sons, neither take their daughters for your sons, and never seek their peace or prosperity, that you may be strong and eat the good of the land and leave it for an inheritance to

your children forever.' And after all that has come upon us for our evil deeds and for our great guilt, seeing that you, our God, have punished us less than our iniquities deserved and have given us such a remnant as this, shall we break your commandments again and intermarry with the peoples who practice these abominations? Would you not be angry with us until you consumed us, so that there should be no remnant, nor any to escape? O LORD, the God of Israel, you are just, for we are left a remnant that has escaped, as it is today. Behold, we are before you in our guilt, for none can stand before you because of this." (Ezra 9:10–15)

The actions of the people in marrying women from the surrounding nations completely contradicted the commands of God. Time in exile had not changed the nature of the idol-worshippers in the surrounding nations. Nor, it seems, had it changed the hearts of the people and made them obedient to this command. Ezra was rightly horrified and scared that these actions would result in God's wrath upon the remnant of the people then in Judah. He understood that the exile was the result of such actions and continuing to sin in this way meant that no one had learned the consequences of sin.

How might we pray this kind of prayer of repentance? It requires first of all that we know the commands of God and the consequences of breaking those commands. Biblical prayer is most often connected to what God has commanded and his redemptive actions for his people. We have the Bible and the more we read it, the more we can see how our lives do not match up to the standard God has set for living as his people. A second way of coming to pray prayers of repentance is to look at the consequences of our sin. The people of Israel were sent into exile for their sin. But this is not the only consequence. God sent his Son into the world to die upon a Roman cross because of our sin. This was a nontrivial act. The consequences of our sin are so great that the only remedy was the death of Christ. Without that, eternity in hell would be our only option. If this does not drive us to repentance, then nothing will.

Ezra's prayer of repentance brought other people together to repent of their sins. They came together before the temple and wept, confessing their unfaithfulness to God. There they decided to put away their foreign wives and children. The Levites set up a group to investigate and worked through all the men who had married foreign women (Ezra 10:1–17). In this way the situation was dealt with carefully and thoroughly. This example shows us that repentance is often not merely a matter of praying and confessing sin. It frequently involves working to undo our sinful actions. It sometimes involves the church systematically dealing with the results of sin. But prayer is the first step.

Nehemiah

Nehemiah was also in exile in Babylon. Some of the Jews had returned to Judah but at the beginning of the book, Nehemiah was still working as a cupbearer to the king. Hanani, a brother of Nehemiah, informed him of the dreadful state of Jerusalem (Neh 1:1–3). Nehemiah's first response to this was mourning and prayer. "As soon as I heard these words I sat down and wept and mourned for days, and I continued fasting and praying before the God of heaven" (Neh 1:4). It is easy for our first response to events to be complaining about the state of the world, rather than taking the matter to God in prayer. It is also easy to be more concerned about our own welfare than the state of God's people and the kingdom of God.

Nehemiah's prayer is recorded for us.

> And I said, "O LORD God of heaven, the great and awesome God who keeps covenant and steadfast love with those who love him and keep his commandments, let your

ear be attentive and your eyes open, to hear the prayer of your servant that I now pray before you day and night for the people of Israel your servants, confessing the sins of the people of Israel, which we have sinned against you. Even I and my father's house have sinned. We have acted very corruptly against you and have not kept the commandments, the statutes, and the rules that you commanded your servant Moses." (Neh 1:5–7)

He began with praise of the God of heaven and confession of sin. Although God keeps his covenant with the obedient, the people had not been obedient. Although Nehemiah did not mention the grace of God, this was implicit in the fact that Nehemiah prayed at all, given that he himself was a sinner. God justifies the ungodly who have faith in Christ (Rom 4:5). Coming to God and confessing that we are sinners is a necessary part of taking advantage of God's grace. There is no way to find grace, nor is there justification, if we do not accept our sinfulness. Nehemiah understood this.

Nehemiah's prayer continued. "'Remember the word that you commanded your servant Moses, saying, "If you are unfaithful, I will scatter you among the peoples, but if you return to me and keep my commandments and do them, though your outcasts are in the uttermost parts of heaven, from there I will gather them and bring them to the place that I have chosen, to make my name dwell there"'" (Neh 1:8–9). He reminded the LORD of his word. Clearly, the exiles had already experienced the truth that breaking the covenant would result in exile. However, this word also came with a promise that God would bring them home if they returned to him. God's judgement of sin was not the final word. There was opportunity to turn back to him and experience his favour again. This prayer both reminded God of this truth and reminded Nehemiah that there was hope.

"They are your servants and your people, whom you have redeemed by your great power and by your strong hand" (Neh 1:10). Finally, Nehemiah pointed out that the Jews were in fact God's people, redeemed by God himself. Reminding God of what he has done in the past to make his people his people was a frequent part of recorded prayers of leaders. They asked the God who had already acted on behalf of his people to act again. This assumes that God is committed to his past choices, that is, he is committed to his stated purposes for his people. It also assumes that the God who acted powerfully before has not changed and can therefore act powerfully in the present situation.

Having acknowledged his sinfulness and God's justice in exiling the people of Judah, and reminded the LORD of his promises, Nehemiah then asked for what he wanted. "'O Lord, let your ear be attentive to the prayer of your servant, and to the prayer of your servants who delight to fear your name, and give success to your servant today, and grant him mercy in the sight of this man.' Now I was cupbearer to the king" (Neh 1:11). The pattern of prayer of great leaders is similar throughout. The request is always at the end of the prayer. They establish who God is, what he is like, what he has done in the past, and then request help for the present. In this case, Nehemiah asked at the beginning that God would hear his prayer for the people of God and again asked at the end.

Nehemiah spent days, possibly months, praying for the situation and for help when he spoke to the king. Nehemiah heard about the broken walls of Jerusalem in the month of Kislev (November to December) and yet he did not approach the king with his request until Nisan (March to April). This was a delay of approximately four months. No doubt Nehemiah was biding his time, carefully considering when best to speak to the king. We can assume that Nehemiah spent the waiting time in prayer to the LORD that he would have success with the king. As cupbearer to the king (Neh 1:11), Nehemiah would have been a trusted servant. But this did not make him the king's friend. He needed to be careful that his request did not bring the wrath of the king against him.

Hence, although he had prayed for months beforehand, when the time came, Nehemiah prayed on the spot. When the king saw that Nehemiah was sad, he asked why, and Nehemiah told him about the ruin of Jerusalem (Neh 2:1–3). "Then the king said to me, 'What are you requesting?' So I prayed to the God of heaven" (Neh 2:4). This prayer was clearly silent and quick. There was not time available for Nehemiah to go off into his quarters and pray and then come back. He simply prayed in his head and spoke to the king, telling him boldly what he wanted to do. The effectiveness of this prayer could not and did not stand alone. It was a reiteration of all the prayers of the past months. It would be foolish to think of prayer as only spontaneous. Spontaneous prayer is possible and sensible in many cases, but a disciplined life of regular prayer stands behind the success of spontaneous prayer.

Nehemiah asked that he could return to Jerusalem to rebuild it. He requested letters to the governors of Trans-Euphrates so that he would be given safe passage to Jerusalem. He also asked for timber for the rebuilding. He was given a military escort (Neh 2:5–9), which is different to Ezra, who did not ask for one. This would suggest that there is no rule about this. The answer to Nehemiah's prayer came through the king and the governors. God did not drop wood from heaven. He did not provide an angelic army in this case. It seems unwise to narrow the options of how God answers prayer. He can use pagans to do his bidding and provide for his work.

Once Nehemiah had returned to Jerusalem and had begun rebuilding the walls, opposition arose to the work (Neh 4:1–3). Nehemiah's response to these enemies was not confrontation but prayer. "Hear, O our God, for we are despised. Turn back their taunt on their own heads and give them up to be plundered in a land where they are captives. Do not cover their guilt, and let not their sin be blotted out from your sight, for they have provoked you to anger in the presence of the builders" (Neh 4:4–5). This prayer is interesting because it was a prayer that God would take vengeance on those who hated the Jews. There was no violence or even a reply to the enemy by Nehemiah. He gave over all the hurt to the LORD. The statement, "they have provoked you to anger" implies that ridicule of God's people makes the LORD angry. The prayer also assumed that God can and will act on behalf of his people. There was no desire for forgiveness of the persecutors on the part of Nehemiah.

The enemies heard that the wall rebuilding was progressing well. So, they plotted to fight against the Jews (Neh 4:7–8). "And we prayed to our God and set a guard as a protection against them day and night" (Neh 4:9). Here prayer was not set in opposition to action, nor action in opposition to prayer. The people did both. God is thus not opposed to action as if it contradicted faith. We both give our problems (in this case the violent plots of enemies) to God in prayer and act to prevent those problems from continuing.

Later, the enemies tried a new tactic, discouragement. The wall was completed, and the enemies still wanted to undermine the work of Nehemiah. They sent him a message about a meeting, which he refused. This happened four times. Then, they threatened to tell the king that the rebuilding was a precursor to the Jews staging a revolt. Again, they asked for a meeting and Nehemiah denied all of their claims (Neh 6:1–8). Nehemiah's response was prayer. "For they all wanted to frighten us, thinking, 'Their hands will drop from the work, and it will not be done.' But now, O God, strengthen my hands" (Neh 6:9). Next the enemies tried to make Nehemiah hide in fear, but he refused (Neh 6:10–13). Again, Nehemiah prayed. "Remember Tobiah and Sanballat, O my God, according to these things that they did, and also the prophetess Noadiah and the rest of the prophets who wanted to make me afraid" (Neh 6:14). In response to each of the enemies' tactics, Nehemiah did not let himself get sucked in, but instead he prayed. Prayer is a good response to such things, in place of panic, anxiety or fear.

The walls were completed, and the people had settled back into their homes. At this point, they all joined together to listen to Ezra the priest read from the law (Neh 8).

> Now on the twenty-fourth day of this month the people of Israel were assembled with fasting and in sackcloth, and with earth on their heads. And the Israelites separated themselves from all foreigners and stood and confessed their sins and the iniquities of their fathers. And they stood up in their place and read from the Book of the Law of the LORD their God for a quarter of the day; for another quarter of it they made confession and worshipped the LORD their God. (Neh 9:1–3)

Reading of the law brought about some changes in the Israelites who heard it. They were brought to repentance because it exposed the aspects of the law that they had not obeyed. Fasting, wearing of sackcloth and putting dust on their heads were acts of sorrow for sin. Separation from foreigners was a symbolic and practical way of casting aside idolatry and the infiltration of foreign gods into Israelite society.

Their confession of sin and worship were the direct result of hearing the word of God. Like the prayers of the patriarchs, the word of God was the foundation upon which their confessions were prayed. Our prayers of repentance, faith and worship cannot be based on our subjective feelings about life. The more the Bible is opened, read and explained, the more will follow prayer of genuine repentance, faith and worship. The implication for us as people with ready access to Bibles is that the Bible should be read regularly and often, preferably at least daily. The other significant way that the Bible can impact our prayers is in church. When pastors faithfully and carefully exegete, expound and explain the Bible, this will drive Christians to greater degrees of prayer, confession of sin and praise.

The Levites then led the people in a prayer of praise to the LORD. The prayer worked through the history of Israel from creation to the present moment for the exiles. It began with praise for the LORD as the only God and Creator of everything. He is not merely the only God but the God of Israel, the one who chose Abram and promised to give his descendants the land, a promise he had kept. The prayer recounted the exodus, the giving of the law at Mt Sinai, and provision of food and water in the desert (Neh 9:5–15a).

The prayer of the people did not ignore the sins of their ancestors, even as it listed the faithfulness of God. The ancestors refused to go into the land, did not remember what God had done for them, and decided to go back to Egypt. Even though they sinned, God did not abandon them. He guided them in the wilderness by day with a pillar of cloud and by night with fire. He gave his Spirit to teach them and provided manna and water to sustain them through forty years of wandering (Neh 9:15b–21).

They praised God because he gave them victory over kingdoms, increased their numbers and gave them possession of the land of promise. They were able to defeat the Canaanites and take over all their houses, vineyards and orchards. The people enjoyed God's goodness. But again, the Israelites were disobedient and rebellious. They killed the prophets and God handed them over to their enemies. Even so, God was compassionate and delivered his people. No matter how much the LORD turned the people back to him, they continued to sin and thereby rejected the life that he offered them. By the Spirit, God spoke to the people through his prophets. But they ignored the prophets. Even so the mercy of God allowed his people to continue (Neh 9:22–31).

Having worked their way through the history of Israel's relationship with their God and their dreadful record of disobedience to the covenant, the prayer arrived at the present situation of the exiles.

> "Now, therefore, our God, the great, the mighty, and the awesome God, who keeps covenant and steadfast love, let not all the hardship seem little to you that has come upon us, upon our kings, our princes, our priests, our prophets, our fathers, and all your people, since the time of the kings of Assyria until this day. Yet you have been righteous in all that has come upon us, for you have dealt faithfully and we have acted wickedly. Our kings, our princes, our priests, and our fathers have not kept your law or paid attention to your commandments and your warnings that you gave them. Even in their own kingdom, and amid your great goodness that you gave them, and in the large and rich land that you set before them, they did not serve you or turn from their wicked works. Behold, we are slaves this day; in the land that you gave to our fathers to enjoy its fruit and its good gifts, behold, we are slaves. And its rich yield goes to the kings whom you have set over us because of our sins. They rule over our bodies and over our livestock as they please, and we are in great distress." (Neh 9:32–37)

Here the people appealed to the greatness and the love of their God so that he would listen to their concerns. Even though they admitted that it was righteous of God to punish their sin, they were stilled distressed.

A BIBLICAL PATTERN OF PRAYER: EXPLORING PRAYER IN THE OLD TESTAMENT

The prayer appealed to the promises of God to the patriarchs that the land would belong to Israel. The Jews were in the land and yet they were in slavery and were forced to give the best of their crops and livestock to a foreign king.

The pattern of prayer that is exhibited here is one that looks to the goodness of God in the past, despite the sinfulness of God's people. God had been merciful before. He made unbreakable promises. He is the God who is worthy of praise. And hence, their sinfulness notwithstanding, they were his people and therefore they called upon him for help. For Christians, the history of salvation is this rich and richer still because God has saved us through the life and death of his Son, the Lord Jesus Christ. The promises of God are greater than those given to the Jewish patriarchs (Heb 8:6; 2 Pet 1:4). Our sins may be as grievous, but the forgiveness offered to believers is greater than that given to Israel (Heb 7:25). Hence when we pray, we have far more of a foundation on which to ask for God's help in our time of need.

In the final chapter of the book, Nehemiah prayed several short prayers. "Remember me, O my God, concerning this, and do not wipe out my good deeds that I have done for the house of my God and for his service" (Neh 13:14). "Then I commanded the Levites that they should purify themselves and come and guard the gates, to keep the Sabbath day holy. Remember this also in my favour, O my God, and spare me according to the greatness of your steadfast love" (Neh 13:22). "I provided for the wood offering at appointed times, and for the firstfruits. Remember me, O my God, for good" (Neh 13:31).

These short prayers in Neh 13 (along with one in Neh 5:19) were prayers that God would remember the work that Nehemiah had done. They show that Nehemiah was concerned with the approval of God rather than the approval of his fellow Jews, the government officials who ruled over Judah, or the enemies who tried to undermine him.

What he did, he did for the sake of pleasing the LORD. It is possible that the LORD is the only one who remembers the good that you or I do in our lives. We may never get public recognition or praise. But it is good to look to the honour given by God himself. If we take this as an example given for our instruction, then it is acceptable to pray for God to see and remember the good we do for his people and his kingdom.

Conclusion

To an extent the exile changed the way Jewish leaders prayed. The sobering truth that God punishes sin was driven home by seventy years under foreign rule. Prayer was necessary to even be able to return to the land. Even when some people returned home, they were still dominated by a foreign power. There are prayers of corporate repentance in both Ezra and Nehemiah. These were not simply prayers about the sins of ancestors; the people who had returned to Judah were still partaking of sin. Enemies abounded and leaders prayed for God's intervention so that the returned exiles could conduct their business in peace. Life as a returned exile was difficult and humbling, and this is reflected in the prayers they prayed.

Reflection Questions / Journal Prompts

1. What experiences have you had that have humbled you and changed the way you pray?
2. Sin is so heinous that the only solution was that the Son of God be crucified (Matt 26:36–46). How does this truth change the way you view the sin in your life?
3. Consider what benefits a regular prayer life has. Consider what benefits spontaneous prayer has. In what ways are both of these types of prayer part of your Christian walk?
4. Think of a situation in your life in which ungodly people have tried to pull you away from serving God. Commit this

situation to God in prayer.

Minor Prophets

The final twelve books of the Old Testament are the minor prophets. Some prophesied before the exile and some after the return from exile. Many give us lessons about prayer. Since the books are generally short (hence the moniker "minor"), the lessons from each are not extensive. Because there are similar lessons about prayer found in the minor prophets as those discussed in the books above, I will not include every book, but only those with something distinctive to say.

Amos, the Intercessor

Amos was a prophet to the northern kingdom before the exile. He was set up by God to be an intercessor for Israel for a time. Amos had a vision of swarms of locusts eating the late-ripening crops (Amos 7:1). "When they had finished eating the grass of the land, I said, 'O Lord GOD, please forgive! How can Jacob stand? He is so small!' The LORD relented concerning this: 'It shall not be,' said the LORD" (Amos 7:2–3). Then Amos saw a judgement by fire, consuming both sea and land (Amos 7:4). "Then I said, 'O Lord GOD, please cease! How can Jacob stand? He is so small! The LORD relented concerning this: 'This also shall not be,' said the Lord GOD" (Amos 7:5–6). The third vision was of a plumb line. But this time, there was no chance for intercession and the LORD did not relent. "And the LORD said to me, 'Amos, what do you see?' And I said, 'A plumb line.' Then the Lord said, 'Behold, I am setting a plumb line in the midst of my people Israel; I will never again pass by them; the high places of Isaac shall be made desolate, and the sanctuaries of Israel shall be laid waste, and I will rise against the house of Jeroboam with the sword'" (Amos 7:8–9).

God showed Amos judgements that might take place in order for Amos to pray that they would not. It was not that Israel did not deserve judgement, but that God did not want to be as harsh as he could be. Thus, like Abraham given an opportunity to plead for Sodom and Gomorrah (Gen 18:16–33), Amos was given a chance to plead for Israel. And, like Sodom and Gomorrah, judgement upon Israel was inevitable because their wickedness was too great to ignore.

When it comes to our own intercession, it is possible that God will bring to mind some person who deserves the judgement of hell. Human beings who reject the grace of the gospel will inevitably be cast into the lake of fire (Rev 20:14–15). This would be the destiny of us all if it were not for the work of Christ. However, let us take the opportunity for intercession, so that some may be saved, just as Abraham received Lot's salvation from Sodom. This would not happen if God did not grant us the chance to pray for people. This does not mean that every person we intercede for will necessarily be saved, but some will.

Reflection Question / Journal Prompt

1. Make a list of unsaved people God has brought to mind to pray for. Spend some time in intercession.

Jonah: Petulant Prayer

Jonah was the prophet who did not want to preach God's grace and mercy to Nineveh because Nineveh was the capital of Assyria, the great enemy of Israel. His life in general, including his prayer life, was one of avoidance of his mission and anger when he succeeded.

Jonah tried to run away from God by getting on a boat in the opposite direction to Nineveh. Once he was on board, the seas became very rough. The pagan sailors prayed to their gods, but Jonah did not pray because he was asleep. Consequently, the captain woke him up so that he would pray to his God to stop the storm (Jonah 1:1–6). The worldview of the sailors was one that required prayer when disaster came. They did not pray to the true God, but they knew that they had no chance to survive if some god did not save them. There is no reason to advocate praying to heathen gods, but Jonah knew the living God and simply did not pray. He was a poor example for us here, as much as those whose prayers were to false gods.

Jonah's poor showing was glaringly obvious when the sailors drew lots and discovered that Jonah was the one responsible for the storm. Jonah told them that he worshipped the God who made everything, and the sailors became even more afraid. When Jonah asked to be thrown into the sea so that it would calm down, they did not want to do it. But the situation got worse (Jonah 1:7–13). "Therefore they called out to the LORD, 'O LORD, let us not perish for this man's life, and lay not on us innocent blood, for you, O LORD, have done as it pleased you'" (Jonah 1:14). They threw Jonah into the sea, and it calmed down (Jonah 1:15). "Then the men feared the LORD exceedingly, and they offered a sacrifice to the LORD and made vows" (Jonah 1:16). Here, they explicitly prayed to the LORD. The prayer included a plea for mercy and forgiveness in advance and an acknowledgement of the sovereign power of God. Their worship was now to the living God, even if it was unlikely to be exclusive. Vows are a prayer of promise to God that something will be done or given to him. It is likely the sailors' worship took place on shore, at an Israelite site of worship. Regardless, in all this, they had more reverence for the God of Israel than did Jonah.

Jonah, however, upped his prayer-life game, as it were, when he was swallowed by a large fish. When Jonah was inside the fish, he prayed as if he were in the grave (Jonah 2:2–7) (compare Jesus speaking of the sign of Jonah, referring to his resurrection from death—Matt 16:4; Luke 11:29). There was a repeated refrain about the distress he was in because of what God did. From the vantage point of near death, Jonah came to a place of repentance, consecration and praise. "When my life was fainting away, I remembered the LORD, and my prayer came to you, into your holy temple. Those who pay regard to vain idols forsake their hope of steadfast love. But I with the voice of thanksgiving will sacrifice to you; what I have vowed I will pay. Salvation belongs to the LORD!" (Jonah 2:7–9). Jonah realised that the LORD is sovereign, and his prayer reflected this. God heard Jonah's prayer and Jonah was vomited onto dry land (Jonah 2:10). The answer was as much an indication of the LORD's sovereignty and mercy as was the fact that Jonah was swallowed by a fish.

Disobedience has an allure that sometimes we simply do not resist. In this state of disobedience, avoidance of prayer is the default mode. It was not until the situation became calamitous, when Jonah felt close to death, even in the grave itself, that he prayed. Perhaps you have experienced the desire to run from God, impossible as that is to accomplish, and the accompanying desire to avoid praying. What would it take to turn your relationship with God around? The truth is that sometimes it takes some harrowing event or sheer despair to bring us back to prayer. If this happens, we should regard it as within the sovereign power and mercy of God to bring his people back to his service.

Jonah went to Nineveh and the people of Nineveh repented when he proclaimed the coming judgement upon them. God had mercy and did not bring destruction upon them (at least not at that time, even if he did so later—see Nahum; Zeph 2:13).

> But it displeased Jonah exceedingly, and he was angry. And he prayed to the LORD and said, "O LORD, is not this what I said when I was yet in my country? That is why I made haste to flee to Tarshish; for I knew that you are a

gracious God and merciful, slow to anger and abounding in steadfast love, and relenting from disaster. Therefore now, O LORD, please take my life from me, for it is better for me to die than to live." (Jonah 4:1–3)

Jonah prayed in accordance with God's character, but it was a complaint rather than praise. He was angry that the people of Nineveh repented because he wanted God to judge them. He was angry that God was merciful to the enemy of Israel instead of wiping them out. It is possible, then, to have a strong understanding of God's character and even to express it in prayer, and yet share nothing of what God desires for us to pray. Since God is a God of grace and mercy, do we want to pray for the salvation of our enemies or their destruction?

Reflection Question / Journal Prompt

1. Have you ever attempted to run away from God or from what he has called you to do? What did it take for you to seek him in prayer again?

Habakkuk: A Surprising Answer

Habakkuk is a short book. At the beginning, the prophet Habakkuk asked God a question. "O LORD, how long shall I cry for help, and you will not hear? Or cry to you 'Violence!' and you will not save? Why do you make me see iniquity, and why do you idly look at wrong? Destruction and violence are before me; strife and contention arise. So the law is paralysed, and justice never goes forth. For the wicked surround the righteous; so justice goes forth perverted" (Hab 1:2–4). This was a reasonable question, a question which has probably been asked by many Christians over the centuries. It has been asked in different ways but it comes down to the matter of why evil continues and God does not stop it. Habakkuk received an answer to his prayer, but it was not what he was expecting.

The LORD's answer to the question was that he would do something unbelievable. He would raise up the ruthless Babylonians, people with a reputation for violent conquest. They were rightly feared because of their powerful armies. They were not intimidated by anyone and not stopped by fortified cities (Hab 1:5–11).

Habakkuk responded to this revelation with another prayer. "Are you not from everlasting, O LORD my God, my Holy One? We shall not die. O LORD, you have ordained them as a judgement, and you, O Rock, have established them for reproof" (Hab 1:12). Habakkuk initially praised God, giving him glory as the holy, eternal God, who had sovereignly ordained to punish the wickedness of Judah by using the Babylonians. This was a prayer with solid theology, but Habakkuk seemed unsure that God's plan was a good one. He asked why God would allow a nation more wicked than Judah to punish them (Hab 1:13–17). The LORD replied to this prayer with a promise that those who would come to punish Judah would ultimately themselves be judged (Hab 2:2–20).

Habakkuk then prayed a long prayer of praise, set to music and written like a psalm. "O LORD, I have heard the report of you, and your work, O LORD, do I fear. In the midst of the years revive it; in the midst of the years make it known; in wrath remember mercy" (Hab 3:2). What followed was a song of God's deeds on behalf of his people. The song seems to have drawn on images from many different battles which God fought and deliverances he performed for Israel (Hab 3:3–15). Habakkuk sang this song in anticipation of what God would do in the future. "I hear, and my body trembles; my lips quiver at the sound; rottenness enters into my bones; my legs tremble beneath me. Yet I will quietly wait for the day of trouble to come upon people who invade us" (Hab 3:16). The past acts of the LORD gave Habakkuk confidence that the coming invaders would be judged, and he was able to have peace.

And therefore, Habakkuk could end the book with these famous words of trust in God in the midst of serious difficulty.

> Though the fig tree should not blossom, nor fruit be on the vines, the produce of the olive fail and the fields yield no food, the flock be cut off from the fold and there be no herd in the stalls, yet I will rejoice in the LORD; I will take joy in the God of my salvation. GOD, the Lord, is my strength; he makes my feet like the deer's; he makes me tread on my high places. To the choirmaster: with stringed instruments. (Hab 3:17–19)

Reflection Question / Journal Prompt

1. Have you asked the question of God that Habakkuk asked? What was your response to the answer God gave Habakkuk? How does it compare to Habakkuk's final words?

Zechariah: Hypocrisy Will Turn to Devotion

Zechariah prophesied to the remnant which had come back to Judah from exile. "In the fourth year of King Darius, the word of the LORD came to Zechariah on the fourth day of the ninth month, which is Chislev. Now the people of Bethel had sent Sharezer and Regem-melech and their men to entreat the favour of the LORD, saying to the priests of the house of the LORD of hosts and the prophets, 'Should I weep and abstain in the fifth month, as I have done for so many years?'" (Zech 7:1–3). On the face of it, this seemed like a pious question. They asked about the fast of the fifth month, a time of mourning for the destruction of the temple. Maybe they wondered whether they needed to mourn over the temple, when it had by this point been rebuilt.

The answer to their query came, not through the priest, but through the prophet Zechariah. The answer was probably not what they expected. It is likely that they were trying for a religious ruling on the tradition of fasting. But Zechariah asked whether they really fasted for the LORD or for themselves. He reminded them of what God said in the past, that a true fast is one in which justice is done and mercy shown. The people of the past refused to heed God's word; they would not listen to what God was saying to them (Zech 7:4–12). Hence God was angry. "'As I called, and they would not hear, so they called, and I would not hear,' says the LORD of hosts" (Zech 7:13). Those people were sent into exile (Zech 7:14).

Although the punishment discussed in this passage referred to the exile of Judah to Babylon, a past event for the returned exiles, this was instructive for the people in their present. The character of God had not changed. The hearts of the people apparently had not changed either. Hence their question about fasting for the temple turned out to be hypocritical. They had gone through the motions of showing love for God's temple, while at the same time disregarding his words of command to them regarding justice and mercy. This is no less applicable to us today than it was then. If we want to inquire of God or seek his favour, this will be to no avail if our hearts are set on ignoring the commands of God. He does not listen to those who do not listen to him.

The later chapters of Zechariah contain some eschatological promises regarding Judah and a renewed relationship with God. Relationship with the living God will extend to the nations around Israel, not just those within it. In the end times, God will bless his people and bring them back from where they are scattered. The LORD will be present in Jerusalem and the fasts will turn to festivals of joy (Zech 8:1–19). "'Thus says the LORD of hosts: Peoples shall yet come, even the inhabitants of many cities. The inhabitants of one city shall go to another, saying, "Let us go at once to entreat the favour of the LORD and to seek the LORD of hosts; I myself am going." Many peoples and strong nations shall come to seek the LORD of hosts in Jerusalem and to entreat the favour of the LORD'" (Zech 8:20–22). Here is an end-time promise that the nations will go to seek the LORD and his favour. The end times will be characterised by prayer to the living God. In the New Testament we see a fulfilment of this promise. Christ is our peace, the one who unites both Jew and Gentile into his body, and gives both access to the Father in the Holy Spirit (Eph 2:11–22). Thus the church is composed of peoples from all nations, and all nations come to God in prayer. Prayer is a significant part of relationship with the true God.

Reflection Question / Journal Prompt

1. The prayer in the beginning of Zechariah is hypocritical but later there is a promise of a future when all nations desire to pray to the LORD. Consider how this transformation gives you hope for change in your own prayer life.

Conclusion

Just because they are called *minor* prophets does not mean they have nothing to say to us. The four minor prophets explored in this chapter each teach a different lesson about prayer. Amos was granted the place of an intercessor for the people of Israel. Jonah was humbled, brought to repentance in the belly of the big fish, and yet (wrongly) still felt it necessary to complain about God's mercy. Habakkuk received an unexpected answer to his prayer, and he submitted his thinking to God's ways. Zechariah knew that the people asking for prayer were hypocrites, yet he also knew that the LORD would transform hearts in the future. In our prayer lives, we have the opportunity to intercede for the lost, repent of our rebelliousness, submit our thinking to God's word, and praise God that he will transform hearts in the future in contrast to our present hypocrisy.

A Final Word

The journey of learning about prayer in the Old Testament has been a long one. There are many examples of great prayers but also many examples of people who failed to pray (with dreadful consequences). It is difficult to absorb all that the Old Testament has to say to us about prayer all in one hit. I do not claim to have included everything that might have been said about prayer in its pages. Nonetheless, there are some significant themes that run through the Old Testament, which I will comment on by way of conclusion.

There is one true God, who created the world. He made human beings to be in relationship with him, and prayer is a major part of that. Consequently, we must pray to him alone. However, idol worship was a recurring issue in ancient Israel. This is the default kind of prayer for sinners, as is evidenced from the tower of Babel onwards. Human beings love to make up their own religions. There are many promises about the future of prayer when people will cast aside their idols and pray to the living God. The Old Testament never sees the fulfilment of these promises. Fulfilment is found in Christ, but even so these promises will not be completed until Christ returns.

The history of Israel given to us in the Old Testament centres on particular people whom God chose. We are given few examples of prayer from ordinary people. Those who pray are mainly leaders: patriarchs, judges, prophets, priests and kings. A few individuals who do not fall into these categories prayed, but they are the exception to the rule. Additionally, many prayer requests were made through the mediation of prophet or priest. This underscores the sheer wonder and privilege of Christian prayer. Even though most of us are not Christian leaders or great people in the eyes of the world, through our Lord Jesus

Christ we can come to God in prayer, daily, even hourly. We have no need of a mediator other than Jesus. We can even call God "Father".

Those who are outside of God's covenant with his people have no right to pray. Abraham prayed for Abimelech, Moses prayed for Pharaoh, and Elisha prayed for the Gentile woman. Most of the church in Australia are Gentiles. Under the old covenant we would have had no status at all and no right to be heard by God. This has changed because of Christ. The status of believing Gentiles under the new covenant is the same as that of believing Jews. Again, the privilege of Christian prayer is a privilege for both Jew and Gentile.

God's word is foundational to the prayers of God's people. Many times in Scripture, we are given examples of people who prayed because God spoke directly to them. Other times, they prayed on the basis of God's promises given to the patriarchs or the covenant given to Moses. Godly people did not pray simply based on their own ideas and desires. As Christians, we have God's written word to us, which contains wonderful promises. We have the Gospels, which describe the person of Jesus. It is unlikely that God will speak directly to us, but our prayers can still be a response to God's word given to us.

There are some great prayers recorded in the Old Testament. I have been calling these kingdom prayers because they focus on the wondrous redemptive deeds of the God of Israel. They generally begin with the exodus and recount the times when God rescued his people from their enemies. They also rehearse the constant rebellion and sinfulness of the nation, despite God's great deliverance. They remember the LORD's punishment of sin, but also his patience and mercy. These prayers contain requests based on God's character and past actions. Such prayers are a great example for us as Christians. It is always helpful to base our prayers upon God's character and past acts of salvation. It is also important to include contrition for sin in our prayers.

On the other hand, there are some sad examples of people who failed to pray, and the consequences of those failures reverberate through Scripture. Abraham failed to pray before sleeping with Hagar. Joshua failed to pray before making a covenant with the Gibeonites. Many kings failed to pray before going into battle. All of these failures had negative outcomes. If nothing else, we should learn from these failures. Prayer is not merely a privilege given to believers under the new covenant but a necessity. Our failure to pray regularly will impact our families, our finances, our jobs, our calling, our government and our nation. Many people will remain unsaved without prayer. Many churches will fail to grow without prayer. Many situations will not be resolved without prayer. We may never know what God might have done in our lives and in our world if we do not pray.

Moreover, God does not listen to the prayers of the wicked. Who are the wicked and what makes their prayers abhorrent to the LORD? In the Old Testament, two things stand out as things which anger God and cause him to ignore prayer: idolatry and injustice. In Israel and Judah, many people tried to hedge their bets by worshipping the LORD and also the gods of the nations around Israel. But the LORD is not one god among many and he will not listen to those whose allegiance is divided. Injustice seemed to go with idol worship. Much of God's law is about the treatment of the poor, the vulnerable and the marginalised. Those who ignored justice were ignored by God when they prayed. Since God's character has not changed, this situation has not changed.

The LORD, the God of Israel is concerned to demonstrate that he alone is God. Often God answered prayer for the sole purpose of showing heathen kings and nations who he is. His glory motivates him to answer prayer, even when those who pray are not righteous. God is exceedingly merciful. Kings who repented of their wickedness and sought God were rewarded by God answering their prayers and being merciful to them. This says far more about the mercy of God than it does about human repentance. Although we can have no expectation that God will answer the godless, he sometimes does this for his own glory and because of his mercy.

There are levels of depth in the prayer lives of Old Testament saints. Some had very shallow prayer lives, only making requests occasionally. Some were concerned only with getting immediate answers to their problems. Others grew in their relationship with the LORD, progressively learning more about his character and praising him for his greatness. Some of the prophets complained to God about their lives. Others were able to submit their lives to him without complaint. There are decisions and choices to be made about prayer. We can choose to remain at a basic level of prayer, sometimes asking God for something. Or we can choose to work to deepen our prayer lives through time in the word of God and praise of God, leading to greater trust and even more prayer.

Prayer is part of a relationship with the living God. Such a relationship is based on faith and obedience to God. It is possible to start out with a good relationship to the God of Israel and for that relationship to be disrupted by poor decisions, sin or idol worship. Some of the people we have examined in the Old Testament were godly in the beginning but later drifted away. Some went through the motions of prayer without real relationship with the God of Israel. Yet sometimes wicked people come back to God. Prayer, then, is a choice and one which we need to continually make if our relationship with God is to continue to be a good one.

A BIBLICAL PATTERN OF PRAYER: EXPLORING PRAYER IN THE OLD TESTAMENT

It is tempting to look for a prayer formula. If we had such a formula, we would be able to pray the right words in the right form and always be sure that God would answer us positively. Although there are patterns of prayer in the Old Testament, it is not true that a formula exists that will make God answer our prayers the way we desire. To believe that such a formula exists is to make a fundamental mistake. For such a formula to exist would imply that God is finite and able to be manipulated. But the God we worship is an infinite God, a God who has no need of anyone or anything. He is complete in himself. The reason that he answers prayer is because he chooses to be in covenant relationship with people. This was the case with Abraham, Isaac and Jacob, and subsequently with the nation of Israel. It is still the case. When God calls people to himself in the gospel, he commits to relationship with those people. The decision to enter into covenant is God's decision rather than ours. Therefore, there is no way to manipulate or coerce God to hear us. For this reason, my focus in this book has been on finding a pattern of prayer rather than a formula.

It seems fitting to end this book with a prayer.

> *Of David.* To you, O LORD, I lift up my soul.
>
> O my God, in you I trust; let me not be put to shame; let not my enemies exult over me.
>
> Indeed, none who wait for you shall be put to shame; they shall be ashamed who are wantonly treacherous.
>
> Make me to know your ways, O LORD; teach me your paths.
>
> Lead me in your truth and teach me, for you are the God of my salvation; for you I wait all the day long. Remember your

mercy, O LORD, and your steadfast love, for they have been from of old.

Remember not the sins of my youth or my transgressions; according to your steadfast love remember me, for the sake of your goodness, O LORD! (Ps 25:1–7)

About the Author

Jennifer Cox has been a believer in Jesus Christ since 1982. She has a PhD in theology and is the author of several theological books and articles. Dr Cox seeks to provide theological resources for the church. She has one passion in life, to see Christ exalted to the centre of all things, particularly within the church.

Want to know more about putting Christ at the centre? Look for more of my books on Smashwords (https://www.smashwords.com/profile/view/JennyCox or check out further resources at http://cross-connect.net.au/author/jennycox/).